Cookbook
for
Family
Camping

Cookbook
for
Family
Camping

by Elizabeth Williams

Illustrations: Roland Rodegast

The
Betty Crocker
Kitchens
**have tested
and approved
all of these recipes**

GOLDEN PRESS • NEW YORK
Western Publishing Company, Inc.
Racine, Wisconsin

I dedicate this book to my husband, Carleton Williams, without whom it could not have been finished before 1972, if then. He was a creatively critical taste-tester; he chopped wood for the campfires; he even ate packaged dinners around deadline time, an irony for a cookbook writer's husband.

For one or more valuable suggestions or recipes I thank the following: Nancy Bratt, Ed Espe Brown, Margaret Dilts, Jean Greensfelder, Willa Gritter, Margaret Goldthwaite, Margaret Kibbee, Margaret Kelly, Monica Preisinger, Harriet Rosenthal, Mary Schoen and The Mill Valley S. S. S. (they know who they are).

For help in solving special problems, special thanks are due Carol Eshleman and Beverly Ludwig. The late Hilda Eshleman made many helpful comments and contributed several fine recipes, and I regret that I can thank her only in spirit.

E.W.

Second Printing, 1972

Produced in the U.S.A. by Western Publishing Company, Inc. Published by Golden Press, New York, N.Y. Library of Congress Catalog Card Number: 74–80464.

CONTENTS

INTRODUCTION

The new trend in travel, all around the country, is family camping. Big families and little families, with very small children, with teenagers and in-betweens . . . in sedans, station wagons, tents, campers (rented, most likely), trailers great and small . . . they pack up everything they need for eating and sleeping and set forth.

And why?

Because they can go places which wouldn't otherwise be accessible to them, to mountains and forests and seashores.

Because camping keeps the family together instead of scattering its members to the winds at camps and resorts, leaving the smallest home with a babysitter.

Because they can afford it: no staggering room charges, no enormous restaurant checks for meals the children didn't, as it turned out, want after all.

Because camping means no waiting at airports, no dressing for dinner, very little concern with check-out times and reservations. If a family finds a place they all like, they stay and explore it. If not, they move on.

When the family is all together, with its home on its back, as it were, there isn't the problem of keeping children quiet. There's plenty of room for roaming, and the open sky absorbs vastly more noise than acoustically tiled ceilings could.

Besides the obvious, other wonderful things happen on camping trips. Interests are acquired and developed along the way, in history, geography, geology, botany, who-knows-what. Friendships are struck up with people you couldn't have imagined meeting. Unpredicted camping events become important family memories.

There's more work to family camping than to the packaged tour, but everyone helps, because everyone *wants* to help. This goes especially for the cooking. There's more to it—but everyone's hungrier. There will be mishaps (the broiled steak dropped in the sand—then washed off in the surf; the raccoon that made off with the bacon) and triumphs (the fisherman's wonderful catch of rainbow trout, the clambake so successful it turned into a party for the whole campground).

The recipes to follow use and combine canned foodstuffs, convenience foods, packaged mixes and the good fresh foods of summer (since that's when most families travel). Assuming that good seasoning is to be hoped for, the recipes make considerable use of herbs, spices and sauces. Remember this: four seasonings may add to a list of ingredients, but they take up less than four cubic inches of packaging space and are thrown into the stew in less, *quite* a bit less, than four minutes; yet what they add to the food is not to be measured.

So have a good trip. Eat hearty. Cook easy.

PLANNING AHEAD

The more you plan at home, the more fun you'll have away from home. Good planning doesn't take a lot of time. Just know where you're going (in general), and how long you'll be gone. Then make a list of what you'll need. Check it again another day. Missed something the first time round? Bet you did!

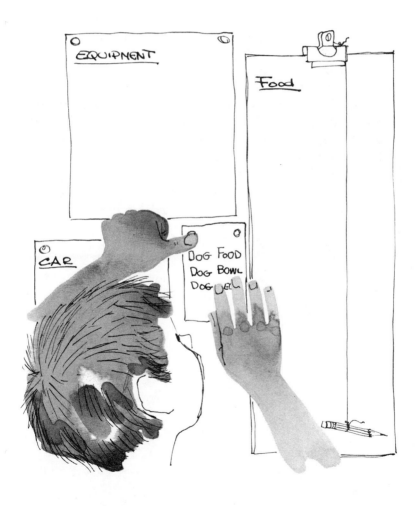

There's no set formula to use in planning the food for a family camping trip because there are so many *kinds* of trips. Each has its special challenges and problems. Your trip might include one, two or all of the situations we'll consider. But plan you must—for whatever type of trip you've decided upon and even with the most elaborate equipment, there are certain specifics to keep in mind.

You'll do all your cooking on a camp stove or over a campfire or charcoal-fed grill. Even with a camp oven or a reflector oven, baking will be limited.

You have to decide what is absolutely necessary—what you can do without and what you can't. Make a list, work it over, and check it when you pack. Forgetting something important can create a real problem. (Imagine canned goods and no can opener.)

Refrigeration, in brief, is primitive. Ground beef, fresh fish, and frozen foods must be used promptly.

Canned goods are easy to use and good to eat—but large cans are bulky and heavy. Remember this if space is a problem.

Your local supermarket is crammed with packaged convenience foods which are not only tasty but lightweight and non-perishable. Many are so new you might not even be aware of them. *Become* aware; they're wonderful traveling companions.

Let the Whole Family Help

If planning food for the trip is a family project, all its members are more likely to be satisfied. Children have strong preferences in foods—and they also have good ideas.

Remember, too, that their unit in Campcraft in the scouting program came around more recently than yours!

Sometimes husbands and children are inclined to be wiser about variety than mothers. If they can eat the same breakfast day after day, the same sandwich lunchtime after lunchtime, why worry about it? Take plenty of what they like but be creative when they want "something different."

The Long Trip

Let's say you're covering a lot of ground. You drive most of the day, find a campsite in the late afternoon (warning: not *too* late, or you might not find one at all!) and settle for the night—or at most two nights—then move on, ever westward. Or eastward, southward or northward, as the case may be.

Breakfast is early, not-too-hurried and hearty. You will want to keep it simple, though, for easy clean-up means a prompt start.

Lunch will be a picnic, probably without cooking, at a roadside park or campground. The emphasis is on refreshment, and the food will be light, cool, fresh, spontaneous. It can be assembled from foodstuffs brought from home and packed in easy-to-reach boxes. Or it can be a treat from a market or roadside stand along the way—or maybe a combination of both. If you're lucky, and alert, you'll find fresh tomatoes, melons, peaches or something else wonderful picked within the last few hours.

During a day of driving, and probably all in the same stop, you'll replenish your supply of ice and buy whatever perishables you'll need for dinner and tomorrow's breakfast: meat, milk for drinking, eggs and so on.

At dinner time you'll be tired from driving all day and busy setting up camp, so you'll want something easy and quick. A one- or two-dish meal fills the bill—and clean-up won't take the kitchen crew's last ounce of strength.

With the day's problems and miles behind you, you can let the children make a campfire and create a really outrageous dessert—and you'll probably eat as much of it as they do!

MEALS ON THE ROAD

BREAKFASTS

FRUIT JUICE (*in serving-size cans*)
CEREAL (*in serving-size boxes*)
POTATO AND EGG SCRAMBLE (*p. 48*)
SWEET ROLLS
COFFEE   MILK

HONEYED GRAPEFRUIT HALVES
HUEVOS RANCHEROS (*p. 46*)
COFFEE   MILK

FORTIFIED FRUIT BEVERAGE (*from powdered mix*)
SAUSAGES AND APPLE RINGS
SOFT-COOKED EGGS
ENGLISH MUFFINS
COFFEE   MILK

LUNCHES

BEAN BONANZA (*p. 54*)
RYE CRACKERS
CHEESE
MELON WEDGES
MILK AND HONEY (*p. 143*)

BORSCHT IN A MINUTE (*p. 56*)
PUMPERNICKEL
CHEESE SPREAD
ICED TEA (*from mix*)

CHEF'S SALAD (*p. 53*)
FRESH BREAD
DELUXE MILK SHAKES (*p. 56*)

QUICK DINNERS

SUNFLOWER CHILI (*p. 71*)
SALSA (*p. 129*)
PEACHES IN FOIL (*p. 149*)
COFFEE   MILK

CHERRY TOMATOES   CARROT STRIPS
LATIN RICE WITH PIZZA SAUCE (*p. 71*)
CHOCOLATE DUMPLINGS (*p. 148*)
COFFEE   MILK

CHICKEN STEW WITH DUMPLINGS (*p. 73*)
DILLED STRING BEANS
MOCK ANGEL FOOD (*p. 150*)
COFFEE   CHOCOLATE MILK

Since you're stopping occasionally, your food plan is made from day to day; it's flexible, even impulsive. But still you're always ready to put together a meal with foods which you have in the car or camper. Remember, though, that if you pass up a promising-looking delicatessen, a sweet-smelling bakery or a creamery full of fine local cheeses, you don't have the idea!

The Long Weekend

Suppose you're driving to a place a few hours from home for a long weekend remote from telephoning, thruways and so on . . . but remote also from the supermarket, the freezer and automatic appliances. You must plan every meal and shop for the whole interval—ahead of time. It's an exercise in descending perishability. The first evening, your main dish is a casserole brought from home, along with fresh vegetables. Next day, you use the frozen foods which you packed in the cooler or ice chest. And finally, you turn to inspired combinations of canned and packaged foods to make the last meal as good as the first!

MEAL PLAN FOR A FOUR-DAY WEEKEND

Thursday Night

DINNER

A CASSEROLE FROM HOME
CORN IN FOIL (*p. 123*)   TOMATOES WITH HERBS (*p. 131*)
GARLIC FRENCH BREAD (*p. 134*)
CAROLINA LEMON POUND CAKE (*p. 42*)
RUSSIAN TEA (*p. 39*)

Friday

BREAKFAST

BAKED APPLES IN FOIL
GRILLED CANADIAN BACON (*p. 93*)
FRIED EGGS
SWEET ROLLS   COFFEE

LUNCH

AVOCADO SANDWICHES (*p. 62*)
READY-TO-SERVE PUDDING (*Betty Crocker's*)
CAROLINA LEMON POUND CAKE (*from Thursday*)
DELUXE MILK SHAKES (*p. 56*)

DINNER

SPAGHETTIOLI (*p. 68*)
MARINATED VEGETABLE SALAD (*p. 128*)
BREAD STICKS
BANANA BOATS (*p. 150*)
COFFEE

Saturday

BREAKFAST

FORTIFIED BREAKFAST BEVERAGE (*from powdered mix*)
EGGS BENEDICT (*p. 49*)
COFFEE

LUNCH

ASSORTED SANDWICHES
COLESLAW (*p. 129*)
ICED TEA

DINNER

SHISH KABOBS (*p. 86*)
FOILED RICE CASSEROLE (*p. 127*)
COUNTRY-FRIED TOMATOES (*p. 126*)
MOCK ANGEL FOOD (*p. 150*)
RUSSIAN TEA (*p. 39*)

Sunday

BREAKFAST

CANNED FRUIT JUICE
BLUEBERRY PANCAKES (*p. 50*)   SYRUP
BACON (*canned*)
COFFEE

LUNCH

CLAM CHOWDER (*canned*) WITH
BACON (*cooked at breakfast time*)
CROUTONS
SLICED ORANGES

DINNER

—But you're home again!

The Week-long Sojourn

If you plan to camp several days in one spot at what might be called a resort area, you can take along staples, seasonings and convenience foods for part or most of the time. There will probably be a grocery or trading post where you can buy meat, milk, eggs and canned goods. Don't count on resort-area stores for hard-to-find items, though. So plan menus ahead, and stock non-perishables. Lunches will be packed for hiking, probably. Dinners can be prepared over campfires, and they can be quick and easy for tired walkers, or lavish and complicated, if there's someone in the party who'd rather cook than hike.

Hot Weather or Cold?

Both equipment and groceries will depend on the weather. If you're going to, or through, a place where it's hot, heavy foods are OUT and cool refreshing foods are IN. You'll be lighting as few fires as possible. Perishables will really perish, and things you don't ordinarily refrigerate will turn limp and gooey if you don't store them in a cool place. An ice chest *and* a cooler are handy.

Cool weather prevails in some of the nicest camping places. Days are mild and the nights downright cold. Here, experienced campers don't bother with an ice chest; they put perishables in waterproof containers and cool them in a stream or lake. For many meals a portable stove *and* a campfire are not amiss. A small stove for heating soups and beverages early and late is a must.

The Overnight Hike

This is a trip-within-a-trip, a jaunt from the car or base camp, more involved than the daytime hike but not so formidable as a long packtrip. The whole family probably shouldn't undertake an "overnight" until they've taken a measure of their stamina with less ambitious walks (and lighter packs).

The main problem, of course, is that everyone must carry food *and* sleeping gear. The very weight and bulk of the pack demand light, compact foodstuffs and cooking and eating equipment.

Each camper should carry his own eating utensils: a plate, a cup and cutlery. The food, much of it premeasured, bagged and labelled, can be distributed among the packs. The same goes for the few utensils needed for preparing dinner and breakfast.

If there's any doubt about the legality or the practicability of making a campfire, take along a portable one-burner stove and fuel. (Sound heavy? There, there . . . a container of "canned heat" weighs $2\frac{1}{4}$ ounces.)

In most areas where this type of trip is popular, plenty of safe drinking water is available. But if there's reason for worry, boil water before you drink it, or use purification tablets, bought beforehand at a drugstore or camp outfitter.

After listing menus (it's really only four or five meals), decide exactly what utensils you'll need. Consider disposable and expendable containers. For instance, you can pack quite a bit of dehydrated food, all nicely bagged in plastic, in a two- or three-pound coffee can. At mealtime, the can becomes a water carrier, then a cooking pot, which can be lifted off the fire with lightweight pliers. Foil pouches and cups are first cooking pans, then eating "dishes." And after you're through you don't wash them; you bury them.

Lunches and snacks eaten on the trail are discussed on pages 58–64. Here are some breakfast possibilities:

ORANGES
GINGERBREAD A L'ORANGE (*p. 147*)
EGGS IN FOIL (*p. 46*)

FORTIFIED BREAKFAST BEVERAGE
(*from powdered mix*)
FRUITED OATMEAL
INSTANT COCOA

STEWED DRIED FRUIT
SOFT CUSTARD (*from packaged mix*)
COFFEE   MILK (*reconstituted*)

And some dinner suggestions:

CLAM-CHOWDERED POTATO SCALLOP (*p. 108*)
COLESLAW
(*dressed with packaged sour cream sauce mix*)
FOIL-GRILLED YELLOW CROOKNECK SQUASH (*p. 125*)
HOT GEL (*p. 144*)

CHICKEN-NOODLE SOUP
FOILED RICE CASSEROLE (*p. 127*)
CHINESE JERKY (*p. 35*)   CARROT STICKS
S'MORES (*p. 148*)   HOT TEA

CREAMED CHIPPED BEEF (*p. 82*)
MASHED POTATOES
(*from Betty Crocker Potato Buds*)
GREEN PEPPER STRIPS
READY-TO-SERVE PUDDING (*Betty Crocker's*)
BEEF BOUILLON

Some of the dishes in these menus, you'll notice, contain whole eggs or foodstuffs that come in small cans. They're fine for a one-night trip, but too much on a longer hike.

One packing tip: a "stick" (¼ pound, ½ cup) of margarine or butter exactly fits into an empty 6-ounce can.

Packing In

The backpacking trip is an extended "overnight." It's what the hunt is to the horseback rider, and it shouldn't be undertaken until you've mastered simpler stages of camping. Families who do it usually become pleasantly nutty about it and spend their winters poring over maps, Forest Service pamphlets and sporting-goods catalogues.

Since planning for a packtrip is specialized, we refer you to the Forest Service booklet, "Backpacking in the National Forest Wilderness" (PA 585), for sale at 15 cents from the Superintendent of Documents, U. S. Government Printing Office, Washington, D. C. 20402.

BASIC EQUIPMENT

What to buy, what to resist buying? What to take, what to leave home? Every family must find its own answer.

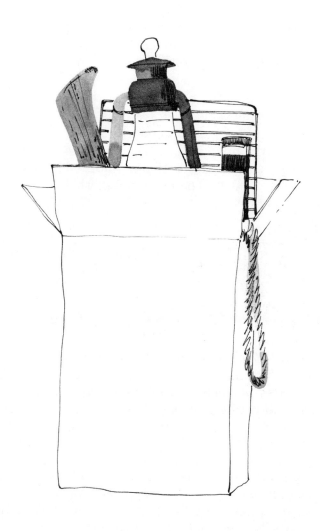

The American family's choice of camping equipment differs almost as much as individual families differ. The Joneses—the ones everybody else is supposed to want to keep up with—have a deluxe three-burner stove, a portable oven, a completely outfitted dropfront cabinet, pots and pans and dishes galore, an ice chest, a cooler, a lantern, a table and chairs, and goodness knows what else. The Smiths have only a grill, two cardboard cartons, a couple of coffee cans and a flashlight. Both, oddly enough, are completely happy. The Joneses like their creature comforts, while the Smiths take pride in their simplicity and ingenuity.

The only conclusion to be drawn from all this is that campers are real individualists, and one camper's absolute necessity is another's white elephant. And that when you're shopping for your own camp-cooking outfit, you would do well to check the salvage shop and the gourmet section of the housewares department as well as the sporting-goods store!

Needed, basically, are arrangements for cooking, refrigeration, cleaning up, storing and transporting foods both staple and perishable; cookware and cooking utensils; dishes and eating implements.

For Cooking

Most—but by *no* means all—families like a two- or three-burner stove fueled by unleaded gasoline, propane or butane. These portable stoves weigh eighteen to twenty-five pounds and fold into what looks like a suitcase.

They can be set up on a station wagon's tailgate, a picnic table, or a special folding stand. One model has folding legs. Most have wind flaps. All kinds go into action quickly and are easy and safe to use. Cooking on them is comfortably similar to using the top burners of your own range.

With or without a portable stove, many families like to have a small one-burner stove along. Hardware and sporting-goods stores can show you a dazzling range of these, all the way from one that costs about a dollar and uses canned "heat" for fuel to a tiny import, a gadgeteer's dream, that sells for around fourteen dollars and burns denatured alcohol. Others, domestic and imported, priced somewhere in between, run on a wide variety of fuels. These—some are called pocket stoves because they are literally small enough to carry on hikes, and, yes, in pockets—are handy for supplementing the bigger stove or campfire at mealtime and for keeping food hot at the table. They are also nice for making the beverage or soup that goes so well with an otherwise cold, dry meal. And if you ask *me,* they're better yet for brewing the eye-opener cup of coffee and the nightcap cocoa or bouillon.

Other kinds of stoves vary so much in size, shape, weight, price and fuel that they defy classification. Some people like an hibachi or other charcoal-burning stove with a grill. There's a small stove that burns newspaper and another that uses almost anything you can pick up off the ground (leaves, bark, pine cones, sagebrush, weeds). Advanced campcrafters know how to make a stove out of a number 10 can or lard bucket. (I haven't tried this, but I'm told it works—it *has* to, or they don't pass the test!)

Most campers don't feel they've really had a camping trip if they haven't done a fair part of their cooking over a campfire. Most roadside campsites have stone fireplaces with grills, and sometimes flat griddle tops. A common problem with these grills is that the bars are often so far apart that pots tip and food falls between them. So it's a good idea to carry your own grill. We like the kind that has four folding, sharp-pointed legs; this can be set on a campsite fireplace, if there is one, or set over a campfire on the ground, if there isn't. (One family takes the wire shelf from the oven of an old kitchen range. In lieu of the folding metal legs, they prop it over the fire with rocks.) A long-handled hinged grill or grill basket also comes in handy.

The subject of camp ovens is mildly controversial. If you have a folding camp oven which can be set on the camp stove or grill, you can bake breads and roast meats. The question is: do you want to? You can heat bread in foil or bake it on a griddle or grill; you can roast or panfry meats in or over a fire. I know of only one camping family that takes an oven with them (they won it in a raffle), but they love it, using it to roast fowl and bake bread from frozen bread dough. *De gustibus* . . .

Reflector ovens are inexpensive, lightweight and compact. They are also, *I* think, for dilettantes at camping . . . you have to learn a special technique for building a special sort of fire, you have to use the fire at just the right stage, you don't stand a chance of baking anything but thin bits of batter or dough. "Why *bother?*" I asked a reflector-oven enthusiast. She replied serenely, "Well, you can say you've done it!"

You can also improvise a reflector oven out of aluminum foil. Here again, advanced campcrafters and veterans of the ruggeder young people's camping programs are the experts to consult.

A few campsites thoughtfully provide electrical outlets. These are not common enough to warrant your loading the car with small appliances as you pack for your trip . . . but it *would* be frustrating to sit there contemplating a place to plug in the electric skillet or coffeemaker that you left at home. You can get advance information on this point and others that may come up as you plan your trip from state and national park services and from associations of private campground operators.

Refrigeration

There are ice chests of many sizes, shapes, and degrees of sophistication, with prices which vary accordingly. Some are simply well-insulated boxes with lids that lift off. Others have latched, hinged doors on the top or the side, which not only keep the cold air in but keep nocturnal visitors (like raccoons and bears) out. There may be trays, compartments with spouts for cold beverages, and shelves. There should be a plug to drain water from melting ice.

Less elaborate and less expensive are lightweight coolers made of molded foam plastic, usually lined with a smooth inside surface. In these you can pack frozen foods (especially the ones in square or rectangular cartons) to use during the first two or three days of your trip.

There is even a universal camp refrigerator which works on electricity, propane or butane. It is neither light nor inexpensive, and it is mentioned here only because it might make a trip possible for a family member whose dietary needs are exacting.

At stores where camping equipment is sold, you can buy packs of "canned ice" which, frozen before you leave home, stay very cold up to five days. Its advantages are that it is completely odorless, gives off no moisture as it melts and can be refrozen and used again. Its disadvantage is that, once thawed, it's useless till next trip.

Clean-Up

No sporting-goods catalogue that I've seen offers a portable dishwasher powered with propane cylinders. *Very* few campsites have hot water taps. Let us face reality. Some families take two plastic dishpans, one for washing and the other for rinsing. Others do the dishwashing in the largest cooking pot, in water heated on the camp stove or the campfire, and rinse at the spring or water tap. In any case, a plastic plate scraper, a dishwashing brush and soaped scouring pads are essentials.

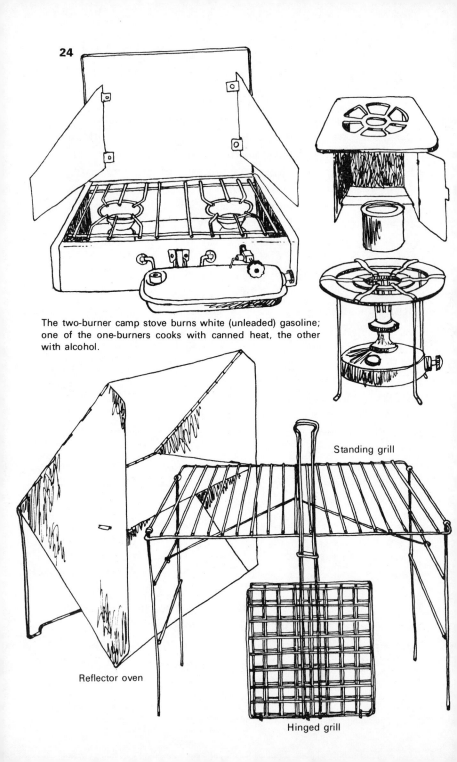

The two-burner camp stove burns white (unleaded) gasoline; one of the one-burners cooks with canned heat, the other with alcohol.

Standing grill

Reflector oven

Hinged grill

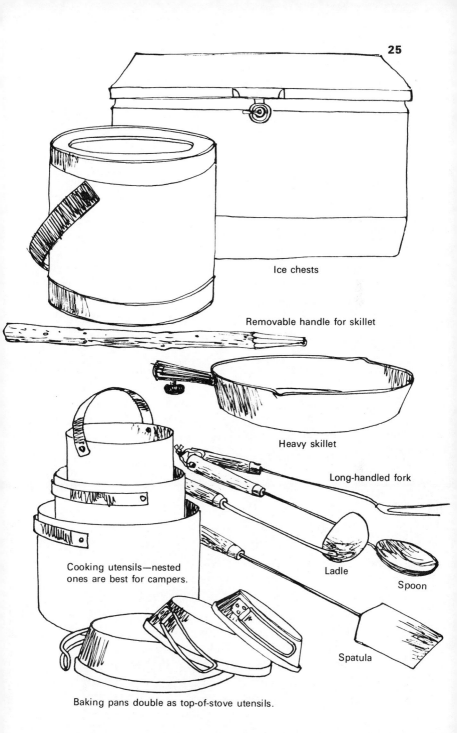

Ice chests

Removable handle for skillet

Heavy skillet

Long-handled fork

Cooking utensils—nested
ones are best for campers.

Ladle

Spoon

Spatula

Baking pans double as top-of-stove utensils.

You can cut down the volume of dishwashing by cleaning utensils as soon as possible after using them; by using paper plates and cups; and by eating foods out of the foil pouches in which they were cooked. It's a good idea to boil the eating utensils every day or so for safety's sake.

The same high, dry air that makes so many camping spots so desirable is very hard on the dishwasher's hands, so consider a pair of waterproof gloves and a good supply of handcream indispensable.

Storage

It is possible to buy or build a camp cabinet designed with a drop lid which doubles as a work surface and with drawers and compartments that let you see what you need when you need it. One precaution—be sure the cabinet doesn't hold *so* much that only a weight-lifter could move it.

Sturdy baskets, preferably rectangular ones, do nicely for carrying foods and cookware. Sturdy, carefully chosen carton boxes—the kind with hand holes—waterproofed with a coat of spray enamel or shellac, make fine pantries. Cardboard dividers between cans and bottles cut down rattles and breakage. I like a tackle box with a compartmented tray that springs up when the box opens for carrying cooking utensils and containers of spices and herbs.

Special hazards in storage for the traveler-camper are these:

—*spilling.* Have a roll of adhesive tape or masking tape handy to seal "easy-open" spouts on cartons of salt, dry milk, and such. A small amount of something like powdered detergent spilled among the foods is quite unpleasant; carry that sort of thing in a container with a tight lid. Make sure bottle caps are screwed on tightly.

—*moisture.* Even if it doesn't rain, the nights (and sometimes the days) are misty. Protect foods packaged in cardboard cartons with foil or plastic coverings, or transfer them to moistureproof containers.

—hungry little (and big) woodland friends. Park and forest rangers can advise you on how to protect your stores against bears. Raccoons have an excellent sense of smell and incredibly clever little hands. Keep foodstuffs under lock or latch, or bagged and tied to a rope line out of reach. Pack rats and certain of their little cousins collect bright little metal objects like beverage-can openers, car keys, and cigarette lighters . . . need I say more?

Cookware and Utensils

Essentials are a good-sized skillet with a good lid, a generous kettle for carrying and heating water, a couple of saucepans, a mixing bowl or two (or, better, a couple of pint measuring cups which easily double as mixing bowls), and a covered pot for heating water and making coffee and other hot beverages. These can be purchased in nesting kits, or you can raid your own kitchen cupboard and add what's missing. (The kits sometimes include a set of metal cups; don't use these for hot beverages, because they get too hot to drink from.) Some sort of colander or large strainer is useful for steaming some foods and draining others. A large metal bowl makes a double boiler of the kettle and doubles as a salad bowl.

I prefer wooden spoons, especially for stirring in metal pots. A cutting board and two or three knives of various sizes are musts; the kind of board which has a slot for a knife is especially useful for traveling.

A long-handled fork is essential as well as at least one pair of tongs, a can opener, an icepick, a vegetable peeler, a grater-shredder, a pancake turner and measuring spoons. A swizzler—a twist of sturdy wire at the end of a wooden handle—does almost as well as a rotary eggbeater and is more compact. A set of skewers is frankly easier to manage than a handful of hand-whittled green twigs. A pair of heatproof mitts goes well, and a metal toasting rack makes toast, besides cooking small fish, hamburgers, what-have-you.

The Picnic Kit

What children, and usually their parents too, like about camp dining is its simplicity. No salad plates, no bread-and-butter plates, no fragile glassware. Veteran campers are likely to have enamel plates, cups, and perhaps soup bowls—simply because that was the kind they got when *they* started going on camping trips. But nowadays lighter-weight, equally durable, plastic dishes are available. They nest for packing, don't rattle, and look nice. Stainless steel "dinnerware"—knives, forks and spoons, to be precise—is ideal. A plastic shaker for mixing the cold beverage, a serving-mixing bowl, and the knife and cutting board can be packed with these in a hamper, along with napkins and a paper or plastic table cover—and that's the picnic kit, always ready to spread for a meal that's small and cool or big and hot.

Extras for the Cook

Two campsites which I've used were especially nice because they had extra work space near the fireplace. In one case there was a waist-high table, in the other a broad concrete expanse next to the fireplace (which I can only assume was a stonemason's error, but I thank him).

To solve the cook's where-to-put-things problem at other campsites one answer is to tie an ammunition belt (from a surplus store) around a tree, slip S-hooks into the holes, and hang pans and utensils there. Another is a shoebag, and still another is a length of clothesline with snap-type clothespins. It's also a good idea to make or buy an apron with lots of pockets to hold cooking tools right where they're needed—on the cook!

GROCERIES FROM HOME

The traveling pantry can be prepared and packed well ahead of time. The hardest part is deciding what to leave at home.

What you take along on your camping expedition will, of course, depend on a lot of factors: how many of you there are and your respective tastes, how much room you have, how long you're going to be gone, and the availability of foodstuffs at your chosen campsite and along the way there.

Your packing also is influenced by the same factors. To me it seems a good idea to start saving receptacles well in advance of the trip—things like coffee cans and little plastic containers. When you put foods in these, label relentlessly on both sides and on the top so you can spot contents quickly.

The following isn't a shopping or packing list, but it may help you make one.

STAPLES

Bisquick—does nearly everything plain flour will and a lot that it won't.

Cornmeal

Cereal for cooking—choose a quick-cooking, highly nutritious kind.

Ready-to-eat cereals—individual-size packages.

Rice—the instant kind is easy to use and so quickly prepared that it's recommended.

Pasta—not the easiest thing to manage in camp, what with the large quantity of water to heat and the draining. The canned kind with sauce is simpler.

Beans—there's a pre-cooked dehydrated kind (hard to find, but available at camping-supply dealers and a few groceries). As for the kinds that have to be soaked and cooked for hours . . . well, *ask* yourself. Canned beans are heavy but handy.

Crackers—there are many flavorful kinds, including the Scandinavian-type whole-grained ones.

Croutons, unseasoned—keep well, are very useful and versatile.

Canned breads

Cornstarch—about ½ cup will thicken several good concoctions.

Pancake mix

FRUITS

Canned—in small-size cans (Avoid leftovers!)

Dried—raisins, apple slices, apricots, peaches, prunes, mixed fruits.

Good keepers—oranges, lemons, grapefruit, firm apples.

VEGETABLES

Canned—beans, corn, beets, tomatoes.

Dried—available in groceries usually as seasoning ingredients or in soup mixes.

Good keepers—carrots, onions, cabbage, turnips.

Potatoes—available as convenience foods (i.e. with seasonings and sauce mixes) for almost every cooking situation. Betty Crocker Potato Buds, Scalloped Potatoes, Au Gratin Potatoes, and Hash Browns with Onions are all light and compact to carry, quick to cook and good to eat.

FATS AND OILS

Margarine—keeps better than butter. There is variation among brands not only in flavor but in melting and softening point.

Salad oil—makes salads, fries and sautés, and enriches many dishes. Choose a good all-purpose, unflavored kind for all-round use.

Mayonnaise or salad dressing—several small jars are handier than one large one.

HIGH-PROTEIN FOODS

Canned meats—plain and seasoned; fish and chicken.

Cured meats—ham, corned beef, jerky, frankfurters. They require refrigeration but keep longer than fresh meat.

Bacon—keeps better if you buy a whole piece and slice as needed. The canned kind is good and needs no refrigeration before it's opened. Bac*Os, cooked bacon-flavored bits of vegetable protein, are available in some areas.

Cheese—dryer kinds keep better.

Cheese spreads

Powdered eggs—available at camp-supply stores. Can be substituted where the fresh taste of eggs isn't an issue, but they don't make satisfactory scrambled eggs.

CONDIMENTS

Catsup or chili sauce
Mustard
Soy sauce
Worcestershire sauce
Pickles and relishes
Canned and packaged soups
Tomato sauce, tomato paste, pizza sauce
Packaged sauce mixes
Grated Parmesan or Romano cheese
Bouillon cubes

BEVERAGES

Coffee—ground, instant or freeze-dried.
Tea—bagged or instant; plain or flavored and sweetened.

Cocoa—instant is much the handier.

Dry milk—perfect for cooking and carrying, even if milk drinkers refuse the reconstituted beverage.

"Creaming" powder

Fruit-flavored fortified beverage mix

Canned fruit and vegetable juices—useful in serving-size cans.

Artificially sweetened drink mix—no nutritive value, but takes the curse off strange-tasting water.

Canned and packaged soups

SWEETENERS AND DESSERTS

Sugar—granulated, confectioners' and brown

Packaged syrup mix

Honey

Jam, jelly, marmalade

Packaged custard mix

Flavored gelatin powder

Betty Crocker's cake, frosting and gingerbread mixes

Betty Crocker's ready-to-serve puddings and ready-to-spread frostings

SEASONINGS AND HERBS

Salt—seasoned salt, garlic salt, celery salt.

Pepper—paprika, cayenne, bottled hot pepper sauce.

Spices—cinnamon, nutmeg, curry powder, dry mustard, ginger (a whole fresh piece if you can get it, ground if you can't), chili powder; sesame seeds, caraway seeds, celery seeds.

Herbs—dried or freeze-dried parsley, chives, basil, marjoram, rosemary, thyme, dill weed, bay leaves, mint.

Dried seasoning vegetables—onion flakes, green pepper flakes.

Garlic or garlic powder

PACKAGED DINNERS

There are too many pre-seasoned one-dish dinners in the market to enumerate. Some are perfect for camp cooking—and some are out of the question. Read the instructions on the package and check these points:

■ Can the dish be prepared with the equipment you have?

■ If you must add ingredients, will they be easily available or easy to store?

■ You can, after a fashion, package your own one-dish dinners. Select a recipe with non-perishable ingredients. Combine dry ingredients and seasonings in a plastic bag. Put this in a larger bag with the canned goods needed to complete the dish. Tuck in a copy of the recipe (or a reference to the page in this cookbook) and label.

Freeze-dried fruits, vegetables, meats and packaged combinations are available at sporting-goods stores. They are good and easy to prepare, but if cost is any object, you might as well treat the family to a restaurant.

UTILITY GOODS

Paper towels and napkins
Facial tissue and toilet tissue
Heavy-duty aluminum foil
Plastic wrap and plastic bags
Washing detergent
Soaped steel-wool pads
Dish towels
Sponge
Matches (in moisture-proof container)

Not on the list are the perishable foods: meat, eggs, milk, sour cream, cottage cheese, baked goods, and many other things you're sure to need or want. These you either take along, carefully packed and chilled, and use while they're still good, and/or buy while you're camping.

To the list you might want to add one or more specialties you make yourself, such as the ones that follow.

CHINESE BARBECUED PORK

2 pounds pork tenderloin
$\frac{3}{4}$ cup soy sauce
$\frac{1}{2}$ cup sugar
$\frac{1}{2}$ teaspoon salt
1 clove garlic, minced
$\frac{1}{4}$ cup catsup

Cut each pork tenderloin into two lengthwise strips. Mix soy sauce, sugar, salt, garlic and catsup; marinate the pork strips in this mixture at least 8 hours.

Drain pork, place it on a rack in a roasting pan or jelly roll pan and bake uncovered for 40 minutes in 350° oven. Cool.

NOTE: This—the Chinese call it *Cha Siew*—keeps well with light refrigeration. It makes good sandwiches; it's also nice to add to cooked vegetables or rice or to substitute for fresh pork or ham in any number of recipes.

CHINESE JERKY

2 pounds flank steak
$\frac{1}{2}$ cup soy sauce
1 clove garlic, minced
1 tablespoon sugar
1 teaspoon salt

Slice flank steak against the grain into pieces about 1 inch thick; cut pieces crosswise into 5-inch strips. (They should be about the size of frankfurters.)

Mix soy sauce, garlic, sugar and salt. Soak the meat strips in this marinade for 30 minutes or longer. Broil on grill about 4 inches from hot coals 4 to 5 minutes on each side. This keeps well with light refrigeration and is delicious as a snack.

6 TO 8 SERVINGS.

PESTO SAUCE

You may *not* substitute dried basil for fresh basil in this Italian classic. Grow some yourself—one healthy plant will provide enough—or ask a resourceful produce man to find some for you.

>   1 cup fresh basil leaves
>   3 cloves garlic, minced
>   3 tablespoons grated Parmesan or Romano
>   cheese
>   3 tablespoons oil (preferably olive oil)

Wash basil leaves and carefully dry them with paper towels; snip them with scissors into a mortar or bowl. Add garlic and grind with a pestle or wooden spoon until basil and garlic are thoroughly crushed and mixed. Gradually add cheese, still grinding. The mixture will form itself into a firm ball. Add oil a little at a time and mix to a pasty consistency. Store in a covered jar or plastic container in a cool place.

And what do you *do* with it? Oh, my!

■ Add a tablespoon or so to 2 cups hot rice.

■ Cook 8 ounces spaghetti according to package directions and drain. Immediately toss with 3 tablespoons Pesto Sauce. Result, the incomparable *Pasta al Pesto.*

■ Slice French bread 1 inch thick. Put one teaspoon Pesto Sauce on each slice; wrap slices in a foil package and heat on grill or camp stove.

■ Broil steaks, hamburgers or lamb chops; smear with Pesto Sauce while hot.

■ Add Pesto Sauce to broiled, fried or stewed tomatoes while cooking.

■ Put a teaspoon of Pesto Sauce in each serving of almost any kind of soup, especially if it's bean or tomato soup or minestrone.

■ Improvise!

PASTRAMI ADLER

3- to 4-pound brisket of corned beef, nicely
    marbled
1 bay leaf
3 peppercorns
1 tablespoon salt
1 tablespoon peppercorns, crushed
1 tablespoon whole cloves, crushed

Put corned beef brisket in a deep kettle and add cold
water to cover. Add bay leaf, 3 peppercorns and salt. Bring
to a boil, then skim; cover, lower heat, and simmer about
3 hours or until meat is tender. Drain meat and place on
a rack. Wrap a plank or cutting board with aluminum foil
and place it on top of the meat; weight with a heavy
object, such as a brick or flatiron. Leave overnight to
extract as much liquid as possible. Next day, mix the rest
of the peppercorns and cloves; rub them into the meat.
Place meat on a rack in a roasting pan and bake 1 hour
in 325° oven.

This keeps well with light refrigeration. Thinly sliced,
it makes good sandwiches and snacks. It can also be used
in the recipe for Creamed Chipped Beef (page 82).

A ROUX FOR CAMPERS

$5\frac{2}{3}$ cups dry milk
2 cups Gold Medal Flour

Mix and store in plastic container, or divide into 7
batches of 1 cup plus 1 tablespoon each and put in plastic
bags.

To make cream sauce, put 1 batch or 1 cup in a saucepan
and add $\frac{1}{4}$ cup margarine, 2 cups water and desired seasonings; stir over medium heat until thickened and
smooth.

FRUITED OATMEAL

6 cups quick-cooking rolled oats
$\frac{3}{4}$ cup dark brown sugar, maple sugar
  or chopped dates
1 cup raisins
1 tablespoon salt

Mix all ingredients and store in a covered container. Use manufacturer's instructions for preparing oatmeal in the desired quantity.

FAIL-SAFE KOSHER PICKLES

Obtain small, crisp pickling cucumbers and foot-long stalks of fresh dill which include the seed heads. Scrub cucumbers and rinse dill stalks. Have ready freshly sterilized pint jars, lids and boiling water. Then, into each jar, first put . . .

1 tablespoon salt
2 cloves garlic, peeled
2 small red chili peppers

Now cram in as many cucumbers as possible. Coil a stalk of dill on top. Fill jars with boiling water to within $\frac{1}{2}$ inch of the top. Seal jars and invert overnight to check for leaks. Leave in a cool, dark place *for at least two weeks.*

NOTE: There's fizzing and bubbling when the jars are opened, but this does not indicate spoilage. Discard dill after opening.

MARINATED MUSHROOMS

36 small mushroom caps
2 tablespoons soy sauce
$\frac{1}{4}$ cup vinegar
3 tablespoons sherry (optional)
2 tablespoons sugar
1 teaspoon salt
$\frac{1}{2}$ cup minced onion

Wash and dry the mushroom caps; put in a quart jar. Combine remaining ingredients in a saucepan and bring to a boil. Pour over mushrooms and marinate for at least 24 hours.

Use as a sort of relish with meat or chicken, in salads or as a filling for omelets.

RUSSIAN TEA MIX

2 $4\frac{2}{3}$-ounce jars orange-flavored instant
   breakfast drink
1 2-ounce jar instant tea
$\frac{1}{2}$ cup sugar
2 .17-ounce packages presweetened lemon-lime
   soft drink mix
1 teaspoon cinnamon
$\frac{1}{2}$ teaspoon allspice

Mix all ingredients and store in a tightly covered container. To prepare beverage, put 1 teaspoon mix in a cup and fill with boiling water.

Does it really cure a sore throat? We aren't sure, but it tastes marvelous!

TASSAJARA SNACK

Guests at Tassajara Hot Springs Resort in California's Big Sur country are given this snack to nibble at rest stops on their hikes in the craggy, scenic country near the resort.

> 6 cups rolled oats (not quick-cooking)
> 2 cups broken walnuts
> 2 cups seeded Muscat raisins
> ½ cup chopped dates (optional)

Toast rolled oats as follows: preheat oven to 250°. Spread rolled oats and walnuts in a roasting pan. Bake 1 hour, shaking pan occasionally. Cool. Mix with raisins and chopped dates. Spoon into plastic sandwich bags or store in a covered container. This is also good as a dessert topping.

48 PORTIONS (about 3 tablespoons each).

NOSEBAG SNACK MIX

> 6 cups Total cereal (8-ounce package)
> ¾ cup brown sugar
> 1 6-ounce package butterscotch bits
> 1 6¼-ounce can Virginia peanuts
> ½ cup margarine, melted

Put Total in a large bowl with brown sugar, butterscotch bits and peanuts. Mix with hands, coarsely crumbling the Total. Sprinkle with melted margarine and toss like a salad, with spoon and fork. Spoon into plastic sandwich bags for individual snacks, or store in a covered container. This is also good to sprinkle on cooked dried fruits.

48 PORTIONS (about 2 tablespoons each).

SWEET SAUSAGE DESSERT

$\frac{1}{2}$ pound margarine
1 pound marshmallows
1 13$\frac{3}{4}$-ounce package graham cracker crumbs
   (about 4 cups)
2 8-ounce packages chopped dates
2$\frac{1}{2}$ cups chopped nuts (walnuts or pecans)
2 4-ounce jars maraschino cherries,
   drained and chopped

Combine margarine and marshmallows in the top of a double boiler and place over boiling water until both are melted, stirring frequently. In a large bowl, mix graham cracker crumbs, dates, nuts and cherries. Add melted margarine and marshmallows; mix well. Pack in 2 well-greased loaf pans. Cover each with a sheet of greased aluminum foil and put in refrigerator for at least a week. Cut loaves lengthwise and wrap in foil. Serve in thin slices.

On the camping trip, this confection travels in your cooler. It's good for snacks and dessert, and a foil-wrapped chunk of it is a great comfort to a hiker.

CAROLINA LEMON POUND CAKE

1 package Betty Crocker Sunkist* Lemon
Cake Mix
½ cup finely chopped nuts, if desired

Heat oven to 350°. Grease and flour a tube pan (10 x 4 inches), bundt pan or 2-quart anodized aluminum mold. Prepare cake mix as directed on package except—use 2 tablespoons less water and stir nuts into batter.

Pour into prepared pan and bake 45 to 55 minutes or until wooden pick inserted in cake comes out clean. Cool 10 minutes; remove from pan. Dust with confectioners' sugar or glaze with Lemon Glaze (recipe below).

LEMON GLAZE

1¾ cups Betty Crocker Sunkist* Lemon
Frosting Mix
2 to 3 tablespoons hot water
1 tablespoon light corn syrup

Blend ingredients in a small bowl. Beat until smooth. (Add 1 to 2 teaspoons water if necessary to make thin enough to pour.) Drizzle over warm cake.

Trademark of Sunkist Growers, Inc.

BREAKFASTS

Quickly and easily cooked, rich in protein and iron, eggs are harmonious in all sorts of combinations. Small wonder that they seem perfect for breakfast, no less so for lunch or supper. And for breakfast, we aren't forgetting pancakes, French toast and variations thereof.

EGGS IN PAPER BAGS

For each person, provide . . .

A sharpened green stick
2 slices bacon
A paper bag, about 4 by 6 inches at the base
1 egg
Salt and pepper

When a small cooking fire is going well, this is the procedure: loop the bacon around the green stick and broil it over the fire. Stop before it's crisp. Shorten bag by cutting or tearing about 6 inches off top. Place the bacon in the bag, making sure the paper becomes saturated with fat. Carefully break the egg into the bag and on the bacon.

Spear the bag with the green stick; hold it about 6 inches above the fire for 2 to 3 minutes or until the egg is done to taste. Tear away the top part of the paper bag, season the egg with salt and pepper, and eat it right out of the bag.

This actually works, however unlikely it may sound.

FRENCH TOAST SCRAMBLE

2 eggs
$\frac{1}{2}$ cup milk
$\frac{1}{2}$ teaspoon salt
4 slices stale bread, cut into cubes (or 3
  cups croutons)
2 tablespoons margarine or bacon drippings

Beat eggs with milk and salt. Pour over bread cubes or croutons and toss lightly. Heat margarine or bacon drippings in a skillet and pour in the bread-egg mixture; fry over medium-high heat, turning occasionally, until browned. Serve with butter and syrup or preserves.

2 SERVINGS.

CREAMED EGGS ON TOAST

$\frac{1}{4}$ cup Gold Medal Flour
$\frac{2}{3}$ cup dry milk
1 teaspoon salt
$\frac{1}{2}$ teaspoon curry powder
1 teaspoon freeze-dried parsley
$\frac{1}{4}$ cup margarine
2 cups water
6 hard-cooked eggs
Toast, English muffins or roll boats

In a saucepan, mix flour, dry milk and seasonings. Add margarine and water and stir over medium heat until thickened and smooth. Peel and finely chop the hard-cooked eggs and add to sauce. Cook, stirring, about 1 minute longer. Serve on toast, English muffins or in roll boats.

6 SERVINGS.

EGGS IN RED

3 tablespoons oil
1 clove garlic, minced
2 8-ounce cans tomato sauce
1 tablespoon onion flakes
$\frac{1}{2}$ teaspoon dried basil
1 teaspoon freeze-dried parsley
8 eggs
Toast or croutons

Heat oil in skillet and sauté garlic until golden. Add tomato sauce, onion flakes, basil and parsley. Simmer 15 minutes, uncovered. Remove from heat.

Break eggs into sauce, spacing them around the skillet. Spoon sauce over eggs; cover and cook slowly 10 to 15 minutes or until eggs are set. Put toast or croutons on plates; top with 2 eggs and a generous amount of sauce.

4 SERVINGS.

HUEVOS RANCHEROS

2 tablespoons minced onion
2 tablespoons oil or bacon drippings
1 28-ounce can tomatoes (3 cups)
1 4-ounce can peeled green chilies, seeded
  and chopped
$\frac{1}{4}$ pound sharp cheese, chopped
6 eggs
6 tortillas

Sauté onion in oil or bacon drippings until soft and golden. Add tomatoes and chopped chilies, then bring to boil. Simmer till thickened, about 20 minutes. Add cheese and stir until melted. Break eggs into the sauce; cover and cook gently 10 to 15 minutes or until eggs are set.

Meanwhile, soften tortillas one at a time by laying over heat on burner or grill about a minute. Put tortillas on plates; top each tortilla with a cooked egg and a generous portion of sauce.

6 SERVINGS.

NOTE: In my vast and zestful experience with canned green chilies I have found that they vary in hotness. That is, the chilies in one can may be pleasantly nippy, while those in another—same product, same brand—blister the tongue and bring tears to the eyes. I therefore make it a practice to take a cautious taste and adjust the amount accordingly.

EGGS IN FOIL

For each serving, make a foil cup about $3\frac{1}{2}$ inches in diameter by molding a 7-inch square of heavy-duty aluminum foil around the end of a one-pound can or similar object. Break an egg into each cup. Set directly on coals and cook to desired doneness. Serve with margarine, salt and pepper to taste.

OX-EYES

1 tablespoon margarine
1 15-ounce can corned beef hash
4 eggs

Melt margarine in skillet. Open can of hash at both ends; push out hash and slice off a fourth at a time. Brown slices in margarine and turn. With back of spoon, make a depression in each slice. Break an egg into each depression. Cover skillet and cook 5 or 6 minutes or until eggs are set.
4 SERVINGS.

SWINGIN' OMELET

4 eggs
2 tablespoons water or tomato juice
$\frac{1}{2}$ teaspoon salt
Dash of pepper
1 tablespoon margarine
Filling (see below)

Break eggs into bowl or pint measuring cup; add water and seasonings. Beat with a fork until yolks are broken and mixture is slightly foamy. Melt margarine in skillet and swing skillet until its entire surface is coated and margarine is bubbly and starting (*just starting*) to brown. Pour in eggs. When the edge starts to set, slide spatula under eggs and tilt pan to let uncooked portion of egg run under. Keep doing this, working from every side. Remove from heat when bottom of egg mass is lightly browned but top is still creamy. Put filling on half of the top; fold the other half over it. Cut in wedges and serve immediately.
4 SERVINGS.

FILLINGS: Slices of sharp cheese and/or tomatoes, crumbled cooked bacon, cooked vegetables, creamed flaked fish, creamed chicken . . . and almost anything else.

POTATO AND EGG SCRAMBLE

3 slices bacon, cut into 1-inch pieces
1 package Betty Crocker Hash Browns with
 Onions
1 teaspoon salt
1¾ cups water
2 tablespoons green pepper flakes
½ cup shredded Cheddar cheese (2 ounces)
4 eggs
1 tablespoon dry milk
¼ cup water
½ teaspoon salt
Dash of pepper

In 10-inch skillet, fry bacon until crisp. Drain bacon on paper towels and pour off all but 3 or 4 tablespoons bacon drippings. Add potatoes, 1 teaspoon salt, 1¾ cups water and the green pepper flakes to the skillet. Cook uncovered over medium heat until liquid is absorbed and bottom is golden brown; turn. Sprinkle with cheese.

Beat eggs with dry milk, ¼ cup water, ½ teaspoon salt and the pepper; pour over potatoes and cheese. Cover and cook over low heat until egg is done and potatoes are golden brown. Cut into 6 wedges and garnish with bacon.

6 SERVINGS.

EGGS BENEDICT

3 English muffins, split in half
Margarine
12 thin slices ham or Canadian bacon
6 eggs
1 10¾-ounce can hollandaise sauce

Toast English muffin halves by laying them face down on grill, then spread with margarine. Lightly fry the ham or Canadian bacon and put 2 slices on each muffin half. Poach eggs in salted, simmering water until set; place on top of ham slices. Meanwhile, heat the hollandaise sauce in a small pan. Spoon 2 tablespoons sauce over each egg.
6 SERVINGS.

NOTE: If you prefer cheese sauce to hollandaise, use a 10¾-ounce can Cheddar cheese soup, following directions on label for cheese sauce.

POTATO BUD CAKES

1 package Betty Crocker Potato Buds
⅓ cup milk
⅓ cup shredded American cheese
2 teaspoons instant minced onion
Margarine

Prepare Potato Buds for 4 servings as directed on package except—reduce water to 1 cup. Stir in milk, cheese and onion. Cool. Shape mixture into 4 to 6 patties. Dip patties into flour or dry Potato Buds; fry slowly in margarine until golden brown on both sides.
4 SERVINGS.

PANCAKES

2 cups Bisquick
½ cup dry milk
1 cup water
1 egg
Margarine
Syrup or jam

Mix Bisquick, dry milk, water and egg; beat with rotary beater or spoon until smooth. Bake on hot, lightly greased griddle, turning when bubbles appear. Serve with margarine and syrup or jam.

ABOUT 18 4-INCH PANCAKES.

Blueberry Pancakes: Add 2 tablespoons sugar to pancake batter; fold in 1 cup fresh or drained canned blueberries.

Cheese Pancakes: Add 1 cup shredded sharp cheese to pancake batter. Serve with creamed meat or vegetables.

Corn Pancakes: Stir 1 cup drained whole-kernel corn into pancake batter. Serve with honey.

Ham Pancakes: Add 1 cup chopped cooked ham or Canadian bacon to pancake batter.

NOTE: For syrup, use packaged instant syrup; or heat 1½ cups brown sugar (packed) with ½ cup water until sugar is dissolved.

ROADSIDE LUNCHES

When you've been traveling most of the morning, and you're hot, and you need to stretch your legs, you want a snack, a refreshing picnic . . . like one of the suggestions on the following pages. Ingredients can be chilled while you ride along or bought at a market or roadside stand and eaten dewy-fresh.

PÂTÉ AUTOMOTIF

½ pound liverwurst (or similar soft liver
  sausage)
Salt and pepper to taste
1 tablespoon sweet pickle relish
¼ cup mayonnaise
1 tablespoon catsup
1 teaspoon prepared mustard
Dash of Worcestershire sauce

Remove casing from liverwurst and put in bowl or on
plate. Mash with a fork and mix in remaining ingredients.
Spread on rye crackers, pumpernickel or other dark,
thinly sliced bread or on raw vegetables such as celery,
carrot sticks and/or cherry tomatoes.
Served thus, this makes a lunch for 4.

NOTE: Fail-Safe Kosher Pickles (page 38) are a fine accom-
paniment for the pâté.

HAM AND MELON ROLL-UPS

2 cantaloupes or 1 Persian or honeydew melon
¼ pound cooked ham, thinly sliced (preferably
  prosciutto, which is admittedly hard to find
  outside Italian delicatessens)

Quarter melon and remove pulp and seeds. Cut the meat
of the melon into chunks about the size and shape of a
finger. Wrap each melon chunk with a slice of ham and
fasten with a toothpick. Serve with cheese-flavored crackers or snacks.
This makes a light lunch for about 4 people.

CHEF'S SALAD

1 large or 2 small heads lettuce (Romaine,
    prizehead or Bibb is preferable, but
    iceberg will do)
1 large or 2 small tomatoes, peeled and
    cut into wedges
2 cups cooked meat (canned lunch meat,
    cold cuts, ham or one of the meats in
    Chapter 3), cut into julienne strips
Croutons (a handful)
1 teaspoon salt
Coarsely ground black pepper
3 tablespoons grated Parmesan cheese
4 tablespoons oil
2 tablespoons vinegar or lemon juice

Wash and carefully dry lettuce leaves; tear into small
pieces and put in a large bowl. Add tomato wedges, strips
of meat, croutons, salt, pepper and cheese. Sprinkle the
oil over all.

Toss lightly until all ingredients are coated. Sprinkle
with the vinegar or lemon juice and toss again. Serve with
good fresh bread cut in thick slices.

6 SERVINGS.

NOTE: You may add chopped green onions, green pepper
and/or cucumber slices. For the oil, vinegar and salt you
may substitute bottled Italian-style dressing. Any of these
ways, it's hard to find a more refreshing lunch.

SHRIMP BOATS

3 large green peppers
3 4½-ounce cans shrimp, chilled
1 cup chopped celery (1 large or 2 medium
   stalks)
¼ cup mayonnaise or salad dressing
2 tablespoons sweet pickle relish
1 teaspoon onion flakes
Salt and pepper to taste

Cut green peppers in half; remove seeds and membranes. Drain shrimp; rinse with cold water and drain again. Combine with remaining ingredients. Spoon salad into green peppers.
6 SERVINGS.

BEAN BONANZA

⅓ cup sugar
½ cup vinegar
½ cup oil
1 teaspoon salt
¼ teaspoon pepper
1 1-pound can green beans, drained
1 1-pound can kidney beans, drained
1 green pepper, finely chopped
1 small onion, finely chopped

In a bowl, mix sugar, vinegar, oil, salt and pepper. Add remaining ingredients and toss together lightly. Serve with dark bread and cheese.
4 TO 6 SERVINGS.

NOTE: Put the cans of beans in the camp cooler a few hours beforehand. You might look for the canned green beans flavored with dill—they make this salad (or any vegetable salad) a special treat.

FRUIT SALAD WITH YOGURT DRESSING

Seedless grapes, stemmed
Cantaloupe or other melon, in balls or small
    chunks
Pineapple chunks, canned or fresh
Fresh peaches, peeled and chopped
1 sprig fresh mint, finely chopped
2 tablespoons lemon juice
2 tablespoons honey
1 8-ounce carton unflavored yogurt

Place fruits—about 4 cups in all, the combination to
depend on what you like best and can get most easily—in
a bowl and sprinkle with mint. Mix lemon juice and honey
with yogurt; pour over the fruit and lightly toss together.
Serve with sweet rolls or slices of canned brown bread or
date-nut roll.

4 TO 6 SERVINGS.

NOTE: The following canned fruits also deserve considera-
tion for this treatment: grapefruit, mandarin oranges,
apricot halves, sweet cherries, green gage plums . . . and
so on, ad infinitum!

BORSCHT IN A MINUTE

1 10½-ounce can beef bouillon, chilled
1 1-pound can shoestring beets, chilled
2 tablespoons lemon juice
1 teaspoon dill weed
½ pint dairy sour cream

Mix all ingredients except sour cream. Serve in cups or bowls; top with a generous spoonful of sour cream.
4 SERVINGS.

DELUXE MILK SHAKES

¾ cup malted milk mix
1 quart milk
1 pint ice cream
Crushed fresh fruit (strawberries,
    raspberries, peaches) to match flavor of
    ice cream, if desired

Stir malted milk mix into milk in a 2-quart pitcher. Add ice cream and fruit, then stir or shake vigorously until ice cream is dispersed throughout.
4 TO 6 SERVINGS.

HIKERS' LUNCHES

*Picnics eaten out of the hamper are one thing; carry-it-yourself
lunches and snacks are quite another story.*

Day-long hikes through, and to, the places where automobiles can't go are—at the time and in memory—the most treasured parts of campers' vacations. Surprisingly small children and surprisingly hoary elders go great distances into the woods, down the beach, up the stream, around the lake . . . loving every minute of it, seeing plants and animals and natural formations that enchant them.

Preparing food for hikers is a cinch, in that each usually chooses and *always* carries his own—and there are no leftovers and no dirty dishes. A knapsack is the classic container for the hiker's lunch; another is a paper or cloth bag tied to the belt with a short length of twine or rope. A good-sized square bandana also makes a fine bag for lunches or snacks—and when the food is gone and the homeward trail seems dusty and dry, the hiker can wet the bandana and tie it around his fevered brow. Whatever the food container, the hiker's hands should be free for swinging along, fishing or gathering "artifacts" as he spots them along the trail.

A hiker's lunch might go something like this:

■ Two or more sandwiches (one or more of meat or cheese, one or more of vegetable and one of something sweet or a sweet-savory combination).
■ A piece of fresh fruit or vegetable or a paper carton of salad or slaw.
■ Dessert: unfrosted cake (frosting is inclined to melt or smear under stress), non-crumbly cookies or candy (not a melting kind).
■ Beverage: One or two serving-size packets of a dehydrated drink mix, and a cup, maybe the collapsible kind.

These should of course be carefully and separately wrapped in waxed paper or plastic wrap and packed so that they won't get crushed.

Be conscious of the danger of food poisoning inherent in carrying highly perishable foods through hot country. Sandwiches made from spreads containing chicken, chopped egg or fish should be made just before the hike, carried in a double wrapping and eaten promptly at lunchtime.

During the hike it's advisable to take a rest stop every hour or so (for city folk, it's absolutely necessary), and at this point a snack is in order. A candy bar may be unimaginative, but it *works*. Other good snacks are a handful of dried fruit, one kind or a mixture of several; a prepared mix (see page 40); a mixture of peanuts, raisins and chocolate bits; a hard-cooked egg; a hunk of cheese; peanut-butter-cracker sandwiches; pieces of raw vegetable. Cherry tomatoes, radishes, carrot strips, cauliflowerets, parsley, watercress, raw spinach and leaves of cabbage or lettuce are all good. (I've always intended, and always forgotten, to imitate the hiker I saw who gathered dandelion greens and miner's lettuce and made himself a little salad by adding French dressing from a tiny medicine bottle which he carried in his shirt pocket.)

While swinging along the trail, some hikers like to chew or suck on something. A hard, sour or highly spiced lump of candy suits some people. Others like chewing gum or a chunk of jerky. I enjoy a little piece of lemon, lime or orange, complete with its nice bitter peel. A man who is an inveterate hiker and mountain-climber assures me that the *perfect* thing is a prune seed. (His wife doesn't agree; she tried it once and pulverized it with her teeth almost at once. She didn't speak to him for miles.)

If sandwiches hadn't been invented yet, we'd have to do it now. Most people have favorite fillings or combinations, some of which other people consider quite eccentric. Variations in the type of bread as well as the filling make a nice change of pace, in the same lunch pack and from one meal to the next. Besides white bread, remember whole wheat, cracked wheat, oatmeal, pumpernickel, Russian rye, egg twist and raisin bread. And the quick breads: orange, banana, prune-nut. And the canned steamed kinds: Boston brown, date-nut loaf.

Any good market has a broad selection of prepared sandwich spreads. In addition, prepared "dips" make new and zestful sandwich spreads.

When you make sandwiches for eating later, beware of wet and soggy bread. Spread it first with margarine, mayonnaise or cream cheese, then add filling. If in doubt, carry filling and bread separately and make your sandwich on the spot. A tomato sandwich is refreshing, but you'd best carry the bread, a tomato and a knife. At lunchtime, you have only to slice the tomato and put your sandwich together.

FOUR "WALKING SALADS"

- Core an apple but leave the blossom end so that the apple is like a cup. Enlarge the core hole and stuff it with cottage cheese. Wrap in plastic wrap or foil.
- Stuff celery with a prepared cream cheese spread.
- Wrap hunks of cheese in tender cabbage leaves.
- Stuff a seeded green pepper with tuna or salmon salad.

SHARP PIMIENTO-CHEESE SPREAD

2 cups shredded sharp Cheddar cheese (about 8 ounces)
1 2-ounce jar chopped pimiento
$\frac{1}{2}$ cup mayonnaise or salad dressing
Dash of hot pepper sauce

Mix all ingredients, adding more mayonnaise, if necessary, to moisten.

For 6 to 8 sandwiches.

EGG SALAD SPREAD

4 hard-cooked eggs
2 tablespoons chopped dill pickle or
   2 tablespoons sweet pickle relish
½ cup mayonnaise or salad dressing
Salt, pepper and paprika to taste

Peel and finely chop the hard-cooked eggs. Mix with remaining ingredients.
FOR 4 TO 6 SANDWICHES.

PIZZA SPREAD

¾ cup oil
1 pound sharp Cheddar cheese, shredded
1 4-ounce can chopped ripe olives
1 8-ounce can tomato sauce
¾ cup minced onion (1 medium onion)

Mix all ingredients. Spread on bread and sauté sandwich in margarine or oil in skillet. Especially good with sourdough French bread or English muffins.
FOR 10 TO 12 SANDWICHES.

CLAM-CHEESE SPREAD

2 3-ounce packages cream cheese
1 7- to 8-ounce can minced clams
2 teaspoons freeze-dried chives
Salt and paprika to taste
3 drops hot pepper sauce

Drain clams, reserving 2 tablespoons liquor. Mash cream cheese with reserved clam liquor. Mix in chives, salt, paprika and pepper sauce.
FOR 6 TO 8 SANDWICHES.

AVOCADO SPREAD

1 fully ripe large avocado
2 teaspoons lemon juice
1 tablespoon oil
1 teaspoon salt
4 slices bacon, fried and crumbled
1 teaspoon onion flakes.

Peel and pit avocado. Mash with lemon juice and oil. Stir in remaining ingredients.
FOR ABOUT 6 SANDWICHES.

CRUNCHY COTTAGE CHEESE SPREAD

$\frac{1}{2}$ pint small-curd cottage cheese
1 green pepper, finely chopped
1 dill pickle, finely chopped
1 tablespoon freeze-dried chives
Salt to taste

Mix all ingredients. Especially good with dark rye bread.
FOR 6 TO 8 SANDWICHES.

IMPERIAL VALLEY SPREAD

2 3-ounce packages cream cheese
3 to 4 tablespoons orange juice
$\frac{3}{4}$ cup chopped dates

Mash cream cheese and gradually work in orange juice. Mix in chopped dates. Especially good with Boston brown bread.
FOR 6 TO 8 SANDWICHES.

CHICKEN-OLIVE SPREAD

3 cups minced cooked chicken or turkey
$\frac{1}{2}$ cup finely chopped celery
$\frac{1}{4}$ cup chopped green olives
$\frac{1}{2}$ teaspoon salt
$\frac{3}{4}$ cup mayonnaise or salad dressing

Mix all ingredients thoroughly.
FOR 8 TO 10 SANDWICHES.

TUNA SALAD SPREAD

1 6$\frac{1}{2}$-ounce can tuna, drained
$\frac{1}{3}$ cup chopped celery (1 large stalk)
2 tablespoons sweet pickle relish
$\frac{1}{2}$ cup mayonnaise
Salt and pepper to taste

Flake tuna and mix with remaining ingredients.
FOR 6 TO 8 SANDWICHES.

NOTE: Salmon salad makes a good spread, too. Substitute
1 cup drained, flaked salmon for the tuna.

SHRIMP SPREAD

3 4$\frac{1}{2}$-ounce cans broken shrimp, drained and
   rinsed
$\frac{1}{3}$ cup finely chopped celery
1 tablespoon lemon juice
1 teaspoon onion flakes
$\frac{1}{2}$ cup mayonnaise or salad dressing

Mix all ingredients
FOR 10 TO 12 SANDWICHES.

MILE-HIGH HAM SANDWICH

1 3-ounce package cream cheese, softened
2 teaspoons brown sugar
¼ teaspoon grated orange peel
2 teaspoons orange juice
6 individual loaves French bread or
    1 1-pound loaf French bread
1 pound sliced boiled ham
1 8-ounce package Swiss cheese slices

Blend cream cheese, sugar, orange peel and juice. Cut bread in half horizontally. (If you use a large loaf, cut it into 6 sections and then in half horizontally.) Spread cut sides of bread with cream cheese mixture. Layer the ham and cheese slices between bread. Wrap each sandwich separately.

6 SANDWICHES.

Some inspiring sandwich combinations

Smoke-flavored cheese spread-bologna
Peanut butter-bacon
Peanut butter-honey-raisins
Peanut butter-catsup (It has great appeal, honestly.)
Cream cheese-watercress-cucumber slices
Cream cheese-spinach leaves
Sliced avocado-onion-catsup
Flaked fish-lettuce-tartar sauce
Mild cheese (Swiss or Teleme)-green chilies
Onion slices-margarine
Deviled ham-chili sauce
Swiss cheese-chipped beef or smoked turkey slices
Canned baked beans-chopped onion
Pastrami-slaw
Cheese slices-sardines-mayonnaise

ONE- AND TWO-POT MEALS

Some of the world's best dishes are the simple, bountiful combinations of meat or fish, artful seasonings and sauces and starch. Traditionally, the cook spends all day preparing such—but suppose she has only an hour or so, and very limited equipment besides? Here are some answers.

RAREBIT-SAUCED STUFFED PEPPERS

1 tablespoon oil
1 teaspoon salt
1⅓ cups boiling water
1⅓ cups instant rice
½ teaspoon pepper
1 teaspoon dried basil
¾ pound ground beef
1 15-ounce can tomato sauce
1 beef bouillon cube
¾ cup boiling water
4 green peppers, halved lengthwise and seeded
1 cup shredded American cheese (4 ounces)

Add oil and salt to 1⅓ cups boiling water; stir in rice. Cover and remove from heat; let stand 5 minutes. Uncover and mix in pepper, basil, ground beef and half the tomato sauce.

In a skillet with a tight-fitting lid, dissolve bouillon cube in ¾ cup boiling water. Add remaining tomato sauce and mix well. Stuff peppers with the rice-meat mixture and place them in the liquid in the skillet. Cover and cook slowly 25 to 30 minutes. Remove peppers to serving plates; add cheese to sauce mixture and heat until cheese is melted. Pour over the peppers.

4 SERVINGS.

PORCUPINE MEATBALLS

1 pound ground lean beef
½ teaspoon salt
Dash of pepper
⅔ cup instant rice
1 tablespoon oil
¼ cup chopped onion
½ cup catsup
¼ cup grape or currant jelly
½ cup water

Mix ground beef, salt, pepper and instant rice. Lightly form into 16 balls. Heat oil in skillet and brown meatballs and onion. Mix catsup, currant jelly and water; pour over the meatballs. Cover and cook over low heat 20 to 30 minutes.

4 SERVINGS.

CAMPOREE CASSOULET

1 pound ground beef
1 cup sliced celery
½ cup chopped onion
½ cup chopped green pepper
1 clove garlic, crushed
1 teaspoon salt
1 1-pound can pork and beans
1 1-pound can lima beans
1 6-ounce can tomato paste

In a large skillet or kettle, cook and stir ground beef, celery, onion, green pepper, garlic and salt until meat is nicely browned and onion is tender. Pour off excess fat. Stir in pork and beans, lima beans (including liquid) and tomato paste. Simmer 10 minutes.

4 TO 6 SERVINGS.

SPAGHETTIOLI

½ pound ground beef
1 6-ounce can tomato paste
1 1½-ounce package spaghetti sauce mix
3 cans (1 cup plus 2 tablespoons) water
1 10-ounce package large-seashell macaroni
¼ cup oil
½ cup croutons (unseasoned)
½ cup grated Parmesan cheese
2 eggs, beaten
1 7½-ounce jar creamed spinach (junior
  baby-food)
1 teaspoon marjoram
1 teaspoon salt

In a saucepan, brown the ground beef. Add tomato paste
and spaghetti sauce mix; stir in water and simmer, uncovered, 20 to 25 minutes.

Cook seashell macaroni in a large kettle of boiling salted
water until tender, 11 to 14 minutes. Meanwhile, combine
¼ cup oil, the croutons, cheese, eggs, spinach and seasonings, mixing lightly with a fork.

Drain macaroni and put it in a bowl (or back in the
kettle). Pour the cheese mixture over it and quickly toss
together while seashells are still steaming hot. Serve with
the tomato-meat sauce.

6 TO 8 SERVINGS.

TOMATO-BEEF CURRY

Since this fine Oriental concoction is so quickly cooked, it's important that you have all the chopped ingredients ready before you begin—no slicing into the pot!

2 tablespoons oil
$\frac{1}{2}$ pound beef (chuck, flank or round), cut
    into $\frac{1}{2}$- to $\frac{3}{4}$-inch cubes
1 bouillon cube (beef or chicken)
$\frac{1}{2}$ cup hot water
$1\frac{1}{2}$ cups fresh tomato wedges (2 large
    tomatoes)
1 green pepper, cut into 1-inch squares
2 medium onions, cut into 1-inch wedges
1 teaspoon curry powder
1 tablespoon sugar
2 tablespoons cornstarch
2 tablespoons water
Hot cooked rice

Heat oil in a skillet. Add beef cubes and cook over high heat for 1 minute, stirring vigorously. Remove beef. Dissolve bouillon cube in hot water. Place tomato wedges in the skillet with the green pepper and onions. Add bouillon; cover and cook 3 minutes over medium-high heat. Uncover and stir in curry powder and sugar. Add beef and, *still* stirring, cook for another minute.

Make a paste of the cornstarch and water; add it to the skillet and cook, *still* stirring, about 2 minutes longer or until sauce is clear and bubbly. Serve with rice.

4 SERVINGS.

CAMPERS' TAMALE PIE

1 pound ground lean beef
1 28-ounce can tomatoes
¾ cup yellow cornmeal
¾ cup cold water
1 tablespoon chili powder (or more, to taste)
1 1-pound can whole-kernel corn, drained
1 4-ounce can chopped ripe olives
Salt and pepper to taste

Brown ground beef in a skillet. Add tomatoes. Mix cornmeal with cold water and add to the meat-tomato mixture by spoonfuls, stirring constantly. Simmer, uncovered, 20 to 25 minutes, stirring occasionally. Add chili powder, corn, olives, salt and pepper; heat through.

4 TO 6 SERVINGS.

BEEF STEW ANDALUSIAN

4 slices bacon, chopped
2 onions, minced
2 cloves garlic, minced
1½ pounds beef chuck, cut into 1-inch cubes
1 cup water
1 6¼-ounce can pitted ripe olives
3 medium-sized potatoes, pared and quartered
1 leek or 2 green onions, chopped
1 strip orange peel
1 teaspoon ground cloves
1 teaspoon dried rosemary
Salt and pepper to taste

In a skillet or kettle, partially cook the bacon. Add onions and garlic; cook until onions are golden. Add beef and brown nicely. Add remaining ingredients; cover and cook over low heat until meat is tender, about 1 hour.

4 TO 6 SERVINGS.

LATIN RICE WITH PIZZA SAUCE

$1\frac{1}{3}$ cups instant rice
$\frac{1}{2}$ teaspoon salt
$1\frac{1}{3}$ cups boiling water
$\frac{1}{2}$ pound bacon, sliced
$1\frac{1}{2}$ cups shredded Cheddar cheese (6 ounces)
$\frac{1}{4}$ cup onion flakes
2 tablespoons green pepper flakes
1 $10\frac{1}{2}$-ounce can pizza sauce

Add instant rice and salt to boiling water in a saucepan. Cover; remove from heat and let stand.

In a skillet, fry 6 slices of the bacon until crisp; drain on paper towels. Chop remaining bacon and fry until crisp. Drain off excess drippings. Add rice to skillet along with shredded cheese; stir until blended.

Sprinkle onion and pepper flakes over rice mixture. Pour pizza sauce over all. Arrange bacon strips on top in spoke fashion. Cover and cook over low heat until cheese is melted. Cut into wedges, each with a strip of bacon.

4 TO 6 SERVINGS.

SUNFLOWER CHILI

8 slices bacon, chopped
4 green onions with tops, sliced, or 1
    tablespoon onion flakes
2 15-ounce cans pinto beans
1 8-ounce can tomato sauce
1 $1\frac{1}{4}$-ounce package chili seasoning mix
1 cup water

In a large skillet, cook bacon; pour off excess drippings. Add green onions and cook slowly till soft. Add remaining ingredients and heat thoroughly. (If you use onion flakes, don't sauté them; add with beans.)

4 TO 6 SERVINGS.

PORK-FRIED RICE

1 tablespoon margarine
1 teaspoon salt
2 cups instant rice (7-ounce package)
2 cups boiling water
4 eggs
1 teaspoon freeze-dried chives
1 teaspoon onion flakes
1 teaspoon salt
1 cup chopped cooked pork, ham or Chinese
   Barbecued Pork (page 35)
3 tablespoons oil

Stir margarine, salt and instant rice into boiling water in saucepan. Cover; remove from heat and let stand 5 minutes. Beat eggs till foamy; mix in the chives, onion flakes, salt and chopped meat. Heat oil in a skillet; when it's almost to the smoking point, pour in the egg mixture and cook, stirring rapidly, less than a minute. Add rice and continue cooking and stirring for 2 minutes longer.

4 TO 6 SERVINGS.

SAUSAGE DINNER

1 package Betty Crocker Scalloped Potatoes
2½ cups water
1 1-pound can sauerkraut, drained
½ teaspoon caraway seed
1 12-ounce package fully cooked smoked pork
   sausage links

Empty potato slices and packet of seasoned sauce mix into a skillet. Add water and heat to boiling, stirring occasionally. Lower heat; cover and simmer 30 minutes or until potatoes are tender. Stir in sauerkraut; sprinkle with caraway seed and arrange sausage links on top. Cover; cook 10 minutes longer or until sausages are heated.

4 TO 6 SERVINGS.

STEW WITH DUMPLINGS

Canned or frozen stew—beef, chicken, veal, lamb
1 cup Bisquick
1 tablespoon dry milk
⅓ cup water
1 teaspoon freeze-dried parsley

Heat stew to boiling in a large saucepan or kettle. Meanwhile, stir up dumpling dough: in a bowl, mix Bisquick and dry milk; stir in water and parsley with a fork. Drop teaspoonfuls of the dough into the boiling stew. Cook, uncovered, over low heat 10 minutes; cover and cook 10 minutes longer.

4 TO 6 SERVINGS.

NOTE: Other herbs may be added to the dough, with or without the parsley. With beef stew, use 1 teaspoon thyme; with chicken, ½ teaspoon rosemary; with veal stew, 1 teaspoon basil; with lamb, 1 teaspoon marjoram.

PORK CHOP SCALLOP

4 rib pork chops, ¾ to 1 inch thick
Bisquick or flour
Salt and pepper
1 package Betty Crocker Scalloped Potatoes
3 tablespoons dry milk
3 cups water

Trim excess fat from chops. Dip chops in Bisquick or flour; brown on both sides in a skillet over low heat. Season with salt and pepper and remove from skillet.

Empty potato slices into skillet; add packet of seasoned sauce mix and dry milk. Stir in water and heat to boiling, stirring occasionally. Reduce heat; place pork chops on top. Cover and simmer 30 to 35 minutes or until potatoes are tender.

4 SERVINGS.

QUICK SCHNITZ UN' KNEPP

2 cups dried apple slices
4 cups water
4 serving-size slices ham, ½ inch thick
1 tablespoon brown sugar
½ teaspoon salt
1 cup Bisquick
1 tablespoon sugar
½ teaspoon nutmeg
Dash of cinnamon
2 tablespoons dry milk
⅓ cup water

Place dried apple slices in a large saucepan or kettle with 4 cups water. Add ham slices, brown sugar and salt. Bring to a boil; simmer, covered, 30 minutes or until apples are tender. Meanwhile, mix the Bisquick, sugar, spices and dry milk in a bowl. Stir in the ⅓ cup water to form a stiff batter. Dipping a teaspoon first into the pot and then into the batter, spoon the batter into the stew. Cook 10 minutes without a lid; cover and cook 10 minutes longer.

4 SERVINGS.

NOTE: This is derived from a Pennsylvania Dutch specialty the very mention of which brightens the blue eyes of the "deitsch" wherever they are. "Schnitz" are the snips of apple, and "knepp"—buttons—are the dumplings. It makes a good breakfast dish, too.

QUICK POLENTA

2 teaspoons salt
4 cups boiling water
1¼ cups yellow cornmeal
1¼ cups cold water
1 1½-ounce package spaghetti sauce mix
1 8-ounce can tomato sauce
1½ cups water
2 5-ounce cans boned chicken, drained
   and chopped
¼ pound Monterey Jack or Swiss cheese,
   sliced

In top of double boiler, add salt to 4 cups boiling water. Mix cornmeal and cold water; add by spoonfuls to boiling water, stirring constantly. Continue stirring over direct low heat until thickened, about 5 minutes. Set over boiling water (in bottom of double boiler) and cook 20 to 30 minutes longer.

In a saucepan, mix spaghetti sauce mix with tomato sauce and gradually stir in 1½ cups water. Add chicken and simmer 20 to 25 minutes. To serve, put a spoonful of hot mush on plate and cover with cheese slices; top with more mush. Spoon chicken sauce over all.

6 TO 8 SERVINGS.

NOTE: If you don't have a double boiler with you, you can improvise with a 3-pound coffee can and a 2- or 1-pound coffee can. Put water and several small rocks in the larger can; set the smaller can inside and cover both with a double thickness of aluminum foil.

HAM AND YAM

1½ pounds boneless cooked ham, cut into
   6 ½-inch slices
⅓ cup soy sauce
1 tablespoon mustard
1 tablespoon brown sugar
1 tablespoon wine vinegar
1 tablespoon sherry (optional)
1 1-pound, 1-ounce can sweet potatoes
1 8¼-ounce can crushed pineapple
½ teaspoon cinnamon
2 tablespoons sherry (again optional)

Marinate the ham 30 minutes in a sauce made of the soy sauce, mustard, brown sugar, vinegar and 1 tablespoon sherry. Broil on grill about 4 inches from hot coals, about 5 minutes on each side.

Meanwhile, mix sweet potatoes, pineapple, cinnamon and 2 tablespoons sherry in a saucepan; cover and heat. Stir to mash smooth with a fork. Season to taste with margarine and salt. Pile sweet potato mixture on freshly grilled ham slices and serve at once.

6 SERVINGS.

MEATS

Meats and campfires have always gone together and they still do. After all, ovens and rotisseries are much newer developments. Here, borrowed from several of the world's cuisines, are ways with meats that take to camping. Don't forget that meats can be marinating while you travel; just make sure the container is leakproof!

Beef

ROAST IN THE COALS

3½- to 4-pound sirloin tip beef roast
  (about 4 inches thick)
1 6-ounce jar prepared mustard (approximately)
1 cup salt (approximately)

Prepare fire so that you have a good bed of hot embers. (It's a good idea to keep a "feeding fire" nearby so that fresh embers can be raked up during cooking.)

Meanwhile, smear entire surface of meat with mustard. Pat salt into the mustard until it will hold no more. Lay the salt-covered meat in the coals and rake embers around it. After about 45 minutes, turn the roast and continue cooking about 45 minutes longer for a rare roast, an hour or more for medium to well done. If you use a meat thermometer (and for this it's a good idea), the meat will be rare at 140°, medium at 160° and well done at 170°.

Remove from coals and knock off the black crust which will have formed. To serve, slice against the grain.

8 TO 10 SERVINGS.

NOTE: You will no doubt have misgivings about this method of roasting beef, such as:

Won't it be too salty?
Mustard with beef?
Won't the coals dry out the meat?

These fears won't be realized. The salt and mustard fuse into a very hot, very black crust, and the meat simply tastes at least as good as the best roast beef you've ever had. And it's delicious cold, too.

BARBECUED FLANK STEAK

1½ pounds flank steak
2 cloves garlic
1 teaspoon dried oregano
1½ teaspoons salt
3 tablespoons oil (preferably olive oil)
2 tablespoons lemon juice or vinegar
1 8-ounce can tomato sauce

Cut flank steak against the grain into strips 1½ inches wide; cut the strips crosswise into serving-size pieces. Place meat in a shallow pan (you can improvise one with foil). In a mortar, bowl or measuring cup, crush the garlic and oregano with the salt, adding oil to form a paste. Rub this into the meat. Drizzle the vinegar or lemon juice over it and let stand an hour or more.

Remove lid from tomato sauce can and set the can at the edge of the grill to warm. Broil the pieces of flank steak on the grill about 4 inches from hot coals, basting with tomato sauce. Cook about 5 minutes on each side.

6 SERVINGS.

NOTE: One camper forgot the tomato sauce but thought it delicious anyway. A comforting thought!

ROUND STEAK KABOBS

1½ pounds round steak, about 1 to 1½ inches
   thick
1 cup wine vinegar
¼ cup salad oil
1 teaspoon salt
1 teaspoon dried thyme
1 teaspoon prepared mustard
½ teaspoon pepper

Cut steak into cubes. Mix vinegar, salad oil, salt, thyme, mustard and pepper. Pour over meat; cover and let stand 6 to 8 hours (overnight, if you like). Thread steak pieces onto skewers. Broil 4 inches over hot coals, turning often, 10 to 15 minutes or until done to taste.

6 SERVINGS.

NOTE: While the meat is marinating, you could be driving, hiking, sleeping . . .

BEEF POCKET STEW

For each serving, provide . . .

¼ pound beef (carry it whole and chop it
   finely at cooking time; or have it already
   ground and *very* cold, even frozen)
1 slice onion, ½ inch thick
1 slice potato, ½ inch thick
1 carrot, slivered lengthwise
Salt and pepper to taste

Shape beef into a patty and place on a 14-inch square of double thickness heavy-duty aluminum foil. Top with onion, potato and carrot sticks. Sprinkle with salt and pepper. Seal foil securely. Cook directly on hot coals 25 minutes, turning once. Eat from foil packet.

BEEF BRISKET BARBECUE

4- to 5-pound well-trimmed boneless beef
  brisket
1½ teaspoons salt
½ cup catsup
¼ cup vinegar
½ cup finely chopped onion (about 1 medium
  onion) or ⅓ cup onion flakes
1 tablespoon Worcestershire sauce
1½ teaspoons liquid smoke (optional)
1 bay leaf, crushed
¼ teaspoon coarsely ground black pepper

Wipe beef dry. Rub with salt. Place on 20x15-inch piece
of double thickness heavy-duty aluminum foil. Combine
remaining ingredients; pour over brisket. Wrap securely in
foil.

Place on grill 5 inches from medium coals. Cook 1½
hours or until tender, turning once. Cut diagonally across
the grain into thin slices. If desired, serve in heated French
rolls or toasted hamburger buns.

10 TO 12 SERVINGS.

CORNED BEEF AND CABBAGE IN FOIL

2 12-ounce cans corned beef
1 head cabbage
$\frac{3}{4}$ cup water
3 tablespoons dry milk
$\frac{1}{4}$ teaspoon coarsely ground pepper

Cut corned beef into 6 portions. Wash cabbage and cut into 6 wedges. Mix water and dry milk. Make six 14-inch squares of double thickness heavy-duty aluminum foil. On each square lay a portion of corned beef and a wedge of cabbage. Pour 2 tablespoons liquid between cabbage leaves in each serving. Sprinkle with pepper. Seal foil securely and place packets on medium coals. Cook 30 minutes, turning once.

6 SERVINGS.

CREAMED CHIPPED BEEF

1 3-ounce package chipped beef
1 $1\frac{1}{2}$-ounce package dry cream of
    mushroom soup mix
$\frac{1}{3}$ cup dry milk
$1\frac{1}{2}$ cups water
1 cup chopped celery (about 2 large stalks)

Chop chipped beef and rinse in cold water to remove excess salt. In a saucepan, mix mushroom soup mix and dry milk. Gradually stir in water. Add chipped beef and chopped celery. Heat until bubbly, stirring constantly. Serve on toast.

4 SERVINGS.

DOUBLE-DECKER HAMBURGERS

2 pounds ground beef
2 eggs
$\frac{1}{2}$ cup bread crumbs
2 teaspoons salt
Dash of pepper
Fillings (below)

Mix beef, eggs, bread crumbs and seasonings lightly; shape into 20 thin patties. On half the patties spread one or more fillings; top with remaining patties and seal edges.

Place on grill 4 to 6 inches from hot coals or wrap individually in squares of double thickness heavy-duty aluminum foil and place directly on hot coals. Cook 15 minutes or until done, turning once. Serve in toasted hamburger buns or with slices of French bread.

Fillings to Mix and Match (everyone makes his own): Dill pickle slices, pickle relish, prepared mustard, catsup, horseradish, chopped onions, tomato slices, Cheddar cheese slices, shredded process American cheese.

Onion Filling: Mix $1\frac{1}{2}$-ounce package dry onion soup mix with $\frac{1}{4}$ cup water.

Peppy Cheese Filling: Combine 2 ounces crumbled blue cheese or 2 ounces shredded process American cheese, 2 tablespoons mayonnaise or salad dressing, 1 teaspoon salt, 1 teaspoon Worcestershire sauce, $\frac{1}{2}$ teaspoon prepared mustard and $\frac{1}{4}$ teaspoon pepper.

BARBECUED CHEESEBURGERS IN FOIL

2 pounds ground beef
1 teaspoon salt
$\frac{1}{8}$ teaspoon pepper
1 1$\frac{1}{2}$-ounce package dry onion soup mix
$\frac{1}{2}$ cup water
6 slices process American cheese
6 hamburger buns, toasted

Mix meat with salt and pepper; shape into 12 patties. Combine soup mix and water; stir until dissolved. For each of 6 packets, use a 12x10-inch piece of heavy-duty aluminum foil. Place a meat patty on each piece of foil; spread with 2 teaspoons onion sauce. Top with a cheese slice and second patty. Press edges of hamburgers together. Spread with another 2 teaspoons onion sauce. Wrap securely in foil. Cook directly on hot coals, 8 to 10 minutes on each side. Serve in toasted buns.

6 SERVINGS.

PIONEER STEAK

Allow $\frac{1}{4}$ pound ground beef per serving. Season to taste with salt, pepper, Worcestershire sauce and a pinch of ground thyme. Shape 3 balls and thread onto skewers or green sticks. Cook over hot coals until done to taste. Serve with rolls.

BEEFBURGER SPECIALS

1½ pounds ground beef
¾ cup soft bread crumbs
⅓ cup milk
¼ cup catsup
1 medium onion, finely chopped
1 tablespoon prepared mustard
2 teaspoons Worcestershire sauce
2 teaspoons horseradish
1½ teaspoons salt

Combine all ingredients; mix lightly. Shape into 6 large patties. Place on wire grill or in hinged grill. Broil 4 inches from hot coals about 7 minutes on each side or until browned outside and medium inside. If desired, serve in toasted hamburger buns.

6 SERVINGS.

TERIBURGERS

Hawaiian drive-in restaurants feature this eclectic blend of Eastern and Western flavors and substances.

1 pound ground chuck
½ cup soy sauce
2 tablespoons sugar
1 clove garlic, crushed
1 teaspoon crushed ginger root or
   ¼ teaspoon ground ginger
4 hamburger buns

Form ground beef into 4 patties and place in a shallow pan or dish. Blend soy sauce, sugar, garlic and ginger; pour over the patties. Cover and leave 30 minutes or longer. Broil on grill 4 inches from hot coals about 7 minutes on each side, basting with the marinade. Serve on hamburger buns with desired condiments.

4 SERVINGS.

Lamb

SHISH KABOBS

2½ to 3 pounds boneless lamb, cut into
   1½-inch cubes
8 onions, peeled
2 green peppers, cut into 1-inch pieces
1 teaspoon dried oregano
Salt and pepper to taste
½ cup dry red wine (optional)
¼ cup vinegar or lemon juice
3 tablespoons oil
8 small tomatoes

Put cubes of lamb (which can be cut from a leg or shoulder roast), onions and peppers in a bowl or a clean coffee can. Sprinkle with oregano, salt and pepper. Mix wine, vinegar and oil; pour over meat and vegetables. Cover and let stand several hours.

To cook, thread the lamb, onions, green pepper pieces and small tomatoes onto skewers. Broil about 4 inches from hot coals 10 to 15 minutes, turning several times.

6 TO 8 SERVINGS.

NOTE: If you use green sticks for skewers, you'll need to make holes in the meat cubes and vegetables before threading them.

ROAST RACK OF LAMB

Rack of lamb, about 3 pounds
2 teaspoons marjoram
1½ teaspoons salt
1 clove garlic
2 tablespoons oil
2 tablespoons lemon juice
2 tablespoons Worcestershire sauce
¾ cup dry red wine

Have butcher saw backbone between center rib bones so it can be cut apart for serving. Trim off excess fat.

In a mortar or small bowl, grind marjoram, salt and garlic; add oil to make a paste. Smear on cut surfaces of the meat. Mix lemon juice, Worcestershire sauce and wine for a basting sauce.

Lay the rack of lamb fat side down on grill about 4 inches from hot coals—and stand by to douse flames from dripping fat. Baste frequently. After about 25 minutes, turn the meat and continue to cook for 15 to 20 minutes, longer if you like it well done. To serve, cut between ribs.

8 SERVINGS.

GINGERED LAMB CHOPS

8 lamb chops (rib or loin), about 1 inch thick
½ cup soy sauce
2 cloves garlic, minced
1 teaspoon minced fresh ginger or ½ teaspoon
  ground ginger
1 teaspoon sugar

Broil lamb chops on grill about 4 inches from hot coals about 8 minutes on each side, basting with a mixture of soy sauce, garlic, ginger and sugar.

4 SERVINGS.

POCKET LAMB STEW

Each camper makes his own, adjusting seasonings to taste. For each serving . . .

1/4 pound boneless lamb, cut into 1-inch cubes
1/3 cup instant rice
1/3 cup water
1 teaspoon onion flakes
1 teaspoon parsley flakes
1/2 teaspoon salt
1/8 teaspoon curry powder
1 small tomato, fresh or canned

Shape a double thickness of heavy-duty aluminum foil into a bowl. In it place cubed lamb, rice, water, seasonings and the tomato. Seal into a pouch and place on hot coals. Cook 30 minutes, turning once.

LAMB KIDNEYS EN BROCHETTE

8 lamb kidneys
4 slices bacon

Cut lamb kidneys in half lengthwise; remove white membranes and tubes. Skewer one end of bacon strip, then half a kidney, then the bacon, then another half kidney, bacon again . . . and so on, so that the bacon runs back and forth around each of 4 pieces of kidney. Turning often, broil 4 inches from coals 15 minutes or until bacon is crisp and kidneys are cooked through.

4 SERVINGS.

Veal

VEAL PARMIGIANO

1 pound boneless veal steak
Salt and pepper
1 egg
1 tablespoon water
$\frac{1}{4}$ cup grated Parmesan cheese
$\frac{1}{4}$ cup dry bread crumbs
$\frac{1}{4}$ cup oil
1 6-ounce can tomato paste
2 cups water
4 teaspoons onion flakes
1 teaspoon salt
$\frac{1}{2}$ teaspoon dried marjoram
$\frac{1}{2}$ pound mozzarella or Swiss cheese, sliced

Cut veal steak into 8 pieces; season with salt and pepper. Beat egg with the tablespoon of water and pour over veal slices, turning them so all sides are coated. Let stand 5 minutes.

Mix Parmesan cheese with bread crumbs; roll veal slices in this mixture. In a skillet with a good lid, heat oil and sauté veal until nicely browned on both sides. Remove veal. In the skillet, mix tomato paste, water, onion flakes, salt and marjoram; bring to boiling point. Return veal to sauce. Lay sliced mozzarella or Swiss cheese on top. Cover and cook slowly about 30 minutes.

4 TO 6 SERVINGS.

POCKET VEAL STEW

1 pound veal, cut into 1x$\frac{1}{2}$x4-inch strips
1$\frac{1}{2}$ cups croutons
1 tablespoon onion flakes
1 tablespoon freeze-dried parsley
1 teaspoon salt
Dash of pepper
1 16-ounce can solid-pack tomatoes

Make four 14-inch squares of double thickness heavy-duty aluminum foil. Divide veal strips into 4 portions and place a portion on each foil square.

Mix croutons with onion flakes, parsley, salt and pepper. Spoon the crouton mixture on top of the meat, distributing it equally among the portions. Top with the canned tomatoes and pour juice from the tomatoes over all. Seal packets and set them on the medium coals. Cook about 30 minutes.

4 SERVINGS.

VEAL SCALOPPINE

1 pound veal cutlets
$\frac{1}{4}$ cup Bisquick
Salt and pepper
$\frac{1}{4}$ cup margarine
$\frac{1}{2}$ cup sherry or $\frac{1}{4}$ cup lemon juice
1 lemon, sliced

Pound veal cutlets with juice can or other blunt object until flattened. Coat with Bisquick seasoned with salt and pepper. Melt margarine in a skillet until bubbly; quickly brown cutlets on both sides. Add sherry and cover skillet. Simmer about 5 minutes. Serve with lemon slices.

4 SERVINGS.

GRILLED VEAL CHOPS

8 veal loin or kidney chops or 4 veal
  sirloin steaks, about 1 inch thick
¾ cup salad oil
½ cup soy sauce
¼ cup wine vinegar
2 tablespoons Worcestershire sauce
2 tablespoons lemon juice
1 tablespoon dry mustard
2 teaspoons coarsely ground black pepper
1½ teaspoons salt
1 teaspoon parsley flakes
2 cloves garlic, crushed

Place veal in shallow pan. (You can improvise one from aluminum foil.) Mix remaining ingredients; pour over veal. Cover pan and let stand in a cool place at least an hour. Broil veal on grill 4 inches from medium coals. Cook 10 to 12 minutes on each side.

4 SERVINGS.

NOTE: Save the marinade—it's good with chicken or lamb.

Pork

SOUTHERN-STYLE BARBECUED PORK

2-pound boneless pork roast
1 clove garlic, minced
4 green onions, chopped (including green tops)
$\frac{1}{4}$ cup margarine
2 tablespoons lemon juice
1 teaspoon minced lemon peel
$\frac{1}{2}$ cup brown sugar
$\frac{1}{4}$ cup vinegar
$\frac{1}{4}$ cup water
$\frac{1}{2}$ cup catsup
1 tablespoon Worcestershire sauce
2 dashes hot pepper sauce
6 hamburger buns

Slice pork roast crosswise into $\frac{3}{4}$-inch slices and slip into a plastic bag. Cook garlic and onions in margarine until soft; add remaining ingredients and mix well, heating only to lukewarm. Pour into plastic bag with pork slices and marinate while fire burns down to medium-hot coals. Place pork slices on grill about 4 inches from coals; cook 20 minutes on each side or until done, basting frequently with sauce. Serve in hamburger buns.

6 SERVINGS.

GRILLED CANADIAN BACON

$1\frac{1}{2}$ pounds Canadian bacon, in one piece
$\frac{1}{4}$ cup orange juice (fresh or canned)
1 tablespoon brown sugar
Dash of ground cloves

Score surface of Canadian bacon with a knife point in a half-inch grill pattern. Place meat on grill about 4 inches from medium-hot coals.

Mix orange juice, brown sugar and cloves; baste meat frequently during cooking. Cook 40 to 45 minutes, turning often.

6 SERVINGS.

PORK CHOPS BRAISED IN APPLE JUICE

4 loin or rib pork chops, about 1 inch thick
Salt and pepper to taste
$\frac{3}{4}$ cup apple juice
Dash of Worcestershire sauce
4 slices lemon

Make two or three $\frac{1}{4}$-inch cuts in fat edges of pork chops to prevent curling during cooking. Heat skillet and grease lightly by rubbing with the fatty edge of a chop. Brown chops on both sides; sprinkle with salt and pepper. Add apple juice, Worcestershire sauce and lemon slices. Cover and simmer 30 to 40 minutes or until chops are well done. Serve each chop with a slice of lemon and a spoonful of pan gravy.

4 SERVINGS.

SWEET-SOUR PORK

The list of ingredients and instructions for this delightful dish looks staggeringly long. Don't be put off; the dish can be thrown together—almost literally—in less than half an hour.

$1\frac{1}{2}$ pounds boneless pork, cut into 1-inch cubes
2 tablespoons soy sauce
1 tablespoon sherry (optional)
2 tablespoons water
1 teaspoon sugar
1 teaspoon salt
2 tablespoons oil
$\frac{1}{2}$ cup brown sugar
1 tablespoon cornstarch
$\frac{1}{2}$ cup vinegar
2 tablespoons soy sauce
$\frac{1}{4}$ cup water
1 $13\frac{1}{2}$-ounce can pineapple chunks
1 green pepper, cut into 1-inch chunks
1 medium onion, cut into 1-inch wedges
1 tablespoon oil
Hot cooked rice

Put cubed pork in a bowl and mix with soy sauce, sherry, water, sugar and salt. Heat the 2 tablespoons oil in a large skillet almost to the smoking point. Pour in the pork mixture and cook over high heat, stirring vigorously, for 8 to 10 minutes or until pork is nicely browned. Remove pork.

In a pint measuring cup or bowl, mix brown sugar and cornstarch. Add vinegar, soy sauce, water and the syrup from the can of pineapple chunks; mix well. In the skillet, heat the 1 tablespoon oil. Put in the chunks of green pepper and onion and stir over high heat about 2 minutes or until the vegetables are tender-crisp. Now add the sweet-sour sauce mixture and continue stirring until the sauce is thickened and clear. Add pork and pineapple chunks and keep cooking and stirring for another minute or two. Serve with rice.

4 SERVINGS.

NOTE: If you've brought along Chinese Barbecued Pork (page 35), you can use it instead of the fresh pork. Chop the barbecued pork into 1-inch cubes. Omit the first seven ingredients and the process of marinating and cooking the pork; simply stir the barbecued pork into the sauce along with the pineapple, just before serving.

BARBECUED RIBS

3 pounds country-style pork spareribs
Salt and pepper
$\frac{1}{3}$ cup orange marmalade
$\frac{1}{4}$ cup lemon juice
$\frac{1}{4}$ cup soy sauce
1 clove garlic, minced
2 teaspoons cornstarch
2 tablespoons water

On a large double thickness of heavy-duty aluminum foil, about 14x18 inches, place the spareribs in a single layer. Season lightly with salt and pepper. Fold the foil over the ribs and seal at edge and ends with a double fold. Place on grill about 4 inches from hot coals and cook 45 minutes, turning foil packet once during cooking.

In saucepan, mix orange marmalade, lemon juice, soy sauce and garlic. Mix cornstarch and water; add to sauce and cook until thickened, stirring constantly. Remove foil packet of ribs from the grill and open. Place ribs on grill or in grill basket. Spoon sauce on each piece and broil about 5 minutes. Turn; spoon on sauce again and broil 5 minutes longer.

4 SERVINGS.

Chicken

CHICKEN BREASTS WITH RICE

4 chicken breasts, about $\frac{1}{4}$ pound each
1 $10\frac{1}{2}$-ounce can cream of mushroom soup
$\frac{2}{3}$ cup instant rice

Lay each chicken breast on an oiled piece of double thickness heavy-duty aluminum foil, about 14 inches square. Mix cream of mushroom soup (undiluted) with instant rice. Spoon the rice mixture over the chicken breasts. Seal the packets and place them on grill 5 inches from hot coals. Cook about 40 minutes or until done, turning once during cooking.

4 SERVINGS.

GRILLED CHICKEN LEGS

$\frac{1}{4}$ cup soy sauce
$\frac{1}{4}$ cup oil
2 teaspoons fresh ginger, minced, or
   1 teaspoon ground ginger
1 clove garlic, minced
2 teaspoons lemon juice
6 chicken legs (drumsticks plus thighs)

Mix the soy sauce with oil, ginger, garlic and lemon juice. Pour over the chicken legs; let them marinate 30 minutes. Broil on grill about 4 inches from hot coals. Cook about 40 minutes, turning and basting with the marinade several times.

6 SERVINGS.

FISH AND SEAFOOD

The fish that's caught or bought and eaten the same day is so good that it's almost reason enough for the trip. Some seashore campers try to cram enough fresh seafood into their vacation diet to make up for a landlocked year. Inland fishermen are equally enthusiastic. But when the fishing isn't so good, canned fish springs into the breach.

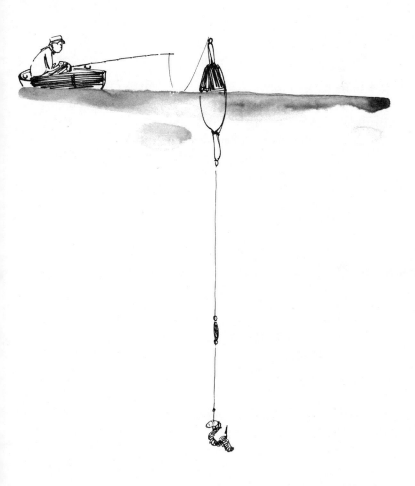

Freshly Bought or Caught

TROUT IN FOIL

Trout or other small game fish
Salt and pepper
Lettuce leaves (large ones)
Bacon
Lemon slices, $\frac{1}{4}$ inch thick

Clean fish; remove scales if necessary. (With trout, it's usually not.) Remove heads and tails, if you prefer. Sprinkle cavity with salt and pepper.

On a double thickness of heavy-duty aluminum foil, about 14 inches square, place a lettuce leaf, then the fish, then 1 slice of bacon, and on top of that 2 slices of lemon. Fold the lettuce over the lemon, then wrap and seal the foil. Cook on medium coals about 15 minutes, turning once.

FISHERMAN'S TROUT

Rainbow, German brown or golden trout,
    up to 8 inches long
Lemon juice
Salt and pepper
Bacon

Clean trout; sprinkle cavity with lemon juice (about 1 teaspoon), salt and pepper. Wrap a slice of bacon around trout. Spear on a sharpened green stick or long-handled fork and cook over coals until bacon is crisp, about 12 minutes. Eat with fingers!

FRIED FISH

Clean trout or other small game fish; scale, if necessary. You may cut off the heads if you like, but leave the tails on. (You're going to eat these with your fingers, and the tail is the handle.) Dredge in Bisquick or cornmeal seasoned with salt and pepper. Fry in oil or bacon fat about ¼ inch deep; brown fish well on both sides and cook until done.

POACHED FISH

Water
1 tablespoon onion flakes
1 tablespoon sweet pepper flakes
1 or 2 leafy tips of celery stalks
1 teaspoon salt
4 peppercorns or 2 dashes hot pepper sauce
Chunks or fillets of large fish (salmon, halibut, swordfish and Ling or rock cod are good)
½ cup dry white wine or 2 tablespoons lemon juice
Canned hollandaise sauce

In a kettle or deep skillet, have enough water to cover pieces of fish. Add onion flakes, pepper flakes, celery tips, salt and peppercorns. Bring to boil and simmer 10 to 15 minutes. Slide fish pieces into simmering water; add wine or lemon juice and simmer 5 to 7 minutes for smaller fillets, longer—up to 25 to 30 minutes—for larger pieces. Fish is done when flesh is opaque and flakes easily when tested with fork. Lift fish carefully from water and place on serving dish. Serve hot with canned hollandaise sauce.

Leftover poached fish makes marvelous salads and sandwiches, too.

GRILLED FISH STEAKS

2 pounds fish steaks (halibut, red snapper,
   salmon or swordfish), $\frac{3}{4}$ to 1 inch thick
$\frac{1}{2}$ cup oil
$\frac{1}{4}$ cup lemon juice
1 teaspoon salt
$\frac{1}{2}$ teaspoon Worcestershire sauce
Dash of hot pepper sauce

Oil a wire grill or grill basket and lay the fish steaks on it. Mix oil, lemon juice, salt, Worcestershire sauce and pepper sauce; brush this sauce over the fish steaks. Set the steaks about 4 inches from medium-hot coals and broil about 8 minutes on each side, basting frequently with the sauce.

6 SERVINGS.

STEAMED CLAMS

Allow about 6 clams for each person. (For real clam lovers, allow 8 or even 12.) Scrub clamshells with a brush, making sure each clam is fresh and alive. (If it's alive, it will close when you handle it.) Put about an inch of water in a kettle or bucket and lay the clams in it. Cover the kettle and bring the water to a boil. Cook 10 to 15 minutes or until clams open. Serve with a bowl—or several bowls—of melted butter for dipping the clams.

(You will notice, perhaps, that I said butter this time. For this, it's worth it.)

CRAB LOUIS

½ cup mayonnaise
½ cup catsup
3 tablespoons oil
1 tablespoon vinegar
½ teaspoon onion flakes
2 dashes Worcestershire sauce
Salt and pepper to taste
1 pound crabmeat
1 small head lettuce, washed and drained

Mix mayonnaise, catsup, oil, vinegar, onion flakes, Worcestershire sauce, salt and pepper; chill. Arrange crabmeat on lettuce leaves and pour dressing over all.
4 SERVINGS.

SHRIMP CHINESE

2 pounds shrimp, raw and in shells
2 tablespoons oil
1 tablespoon sugar
2 tablespoons soy sauce
1 teaspoon salt
2 tablespoons sherry
1 small onion, chopped
2 teaspoons minced fresh ginger
   or 1 teaspoon ground ginger

Wash and drain the shrimp. Heat oil in a skillet; add shrimp and cook, stirring often, for 8 minutes. Stir in sugar, soy sauce, salt, sherry, onion and ginger; cook 1 minute more. Cool. Serve cold.

This keeps two to three days at a cool temperature.
6 TO 8 SERVINGS.

SHRIMP METAIRIE

1 cup butter or margarine
½ cup oil
3 cloves garlic, minced
2 tablespoons coarsely ground pepper
1 teaspoon salt
3 to 4 pounds large headless shrimp,
    raw and in shells

Heat butter or margarine and oil with garlic, pepper and salt in a spacious skillet. (If you're using an electric skillet, use the medium-high heat setting.) When fat is hot but before garlic is browned, add enough shrimp to cover the skillet (about half the shrimp). Cook 7 to 8 minutes on each side. Drain on paper towels.

When all the shrimp are cooked, pour liquid from skillet into a bowl. Serve with hot sliced French bread, which is dipped into the hot butter mixture.

6 TO 8 SERVINGS.

NOTE: Besides being delicious, this is messy (eaters peel their own shrimp)—so provide many napkins. It's thirst provoking, too—so provide plenty to drink. Good accompaniments are mild cheeses and fresh fruit.

OYSTER STEW

½ cup butter or margarine
1 pint oysters
1 quart rich milk
Salt and pepper

Melt butter in saucepan. Add oysters and cook gently until their edges curl. Add milk and heat just until bubbles appear at the edge of the pan; do *not* boil. Season to taste and serve with oyster crackers.

4 SERVINGS.

OYSTER ROLLS

To oyster lovers, this recipe will read like a poem. It's as good as it sounds! A 1-pound loaf of crusty French bread can be used to make one big oyster loaf.

      6 French rolls
      4 tablespoons melted butter
      3 10-ounce jars oysters or 2 pints fresh
      Dash of hot pepper sauce
      1 teaspoon onion juice*
      ½ teaspoon dried tarragon
      ⅓ cup white wine or 2 tablespoons lemon juice

Slice tops off the French rolls and hollow them out with a fork. Shred the scooped-out bread and lightly toast by shaking in a skillet over medium heat. Brush the roll boats with melted butter and lightly toast them also.

In the remaining butter, cook the oysters just until the edges curl. Stir in pepper sauce, onion juice, tarragon and white wine or lemon juice. Add enough of the toasted crumbs to thicken the juice, stirring, and bring just to the boiling point.

Fill toasted roll boats with oyster mixture. Wrap lightly in foil and place on grill. Heat 5 minutes or so. (If you're using an oven, skip the foil wrapping and simply heat the oyster rolls on a baking sheet for 10 minutes at 350°.)

      6 SERVINGS.

*To make onion juice, sprinkle 1 teaspoon salt on the cut surface of an onion. Let stand 5 minutes. Scrape off the juice with a knife.

ROAST OYSTERS

3 dozen oysters in shells
1 cup butter or margarine
1/4 cup cider vinegar

Scrub oyster shells with a brush. Make sure oysters are tightly shut as you handle them (this indicates they're alive). Set oysters on grill about 4 inches from hot coals. Roast 10 to 15 minutes or until shells begin to open. Meanwhile, melt butter or margarine in a saucepan or steel bowl. Add vinegar and stir vigorously with a fork. Diners eat oysters from shells with forks, using the butter-vinegar sauce for a dip.

6 SERVINGS (unless one or more happens to be an oyster fanatic, in which case it might serve only three).

LOBSTER ROAST

Select live lobsters weighing 1 to 1 1/4 pounds each. Allow one per person. Split lobsters in half lengthwise. (This is clearly a man's job.) Remove the dark vein which runs through the center of the body and the stomach, which is just behind the head. Leave the green liver and the coral roe, which are delicacies.

Brush meat surface generously with melted butter or margarine and set half lobsters shell side down on grill about 4 inches from medium-hot coals. Cook 10 to 15 minutes, basting frequently with butter, until the meat becomes opaque. Don't turn during cooking or you'll lose the lovely juices that collect in the shell. Serve hot with lemon wedges, more melted butter or margarine and hot French bread.

NOTE: If you simply can't bear to cope with a live lobster, parboil it in boiling water (enough to cover) for 5 to 10 minutes, then split.

CIOPPINO

1 1½-ounce package Italian spaghetti sauce mix
1 10½-ounce can tomato puree
1 28-ounce can tomatoes
3 green onions, minced (including green
   tops)
1 green pepper, diced, or 1 tablespoon
   sweet pepper flakes
1 teaspoon dried basil
2 dashes hot pepper sauce
2½ cups dry white wine
2 dozen clams, raw and in shells
1½ pounds prawns or large shrimp, raw but
   with heads and tails removed

Mix spaghetti sauce mix with tomato puree and tomatoes in saucepan. Add onions, green pepper, basil and pepper sauce. Bring to boil and simmer, uncovered, 25 to 30 minutes. Add wine and simmer 5 minutes longer.

In a large pot or kettle, arrange the clams, then the prawns. Pour the sauce over shellfish; cover and simmer 30 minutes. Serve with garlic bread.

8 SERVINGS.

NOTE: Other available fish, such as fillet of cod or halibut, and shellfish, such as lobster, lobster tails or king crab legs, may also be cooked in this sauce. This is very messy to eat—since diners shell their own prawns and such—so provide lots of paper towels.

BOUILLABAISSE

Fish heads, tails and backbones
1 bay leaf
1 slice lemon
1 stalk celery, including leaves
1 small onion, sliced, or 2 teaspoons
onion flakes
Water (about 3 pints)
½ cup olive oil
2 small onions, sliced
2 cloves garlic, sliced
2 tablespoons minced celery
2 tomatoes, peeled and chopped
1 teaspoon salt
2 thin strips lemon peel
Pinch of saffron (optional)
2 pounds fish fillets (whatever is available)
Meat of 1 small lobster
¾ pound scallops
1 cup shrimp, cooked and shelled

Make fish stock by boiling fish parts, bay leaf, lemon slice, celery stalk and onion or onion flakes in water 20 to 30 minutes. Remove and discard fish parts and seasonings. In a large pot, heat olive oil and sauté 2 onions, garlic and celery until soft and golden. Add tomatoes, salt, lemon peel and saffron. Add fish stock and boil *hard* for 5 minutes. Add fish fillets, lobster meat, scallops and shrimp; continue boiling hard 5 minutes longer. Place toasted French bread slices in soup plates. Spoon fish over bread and fill plates with broth.

8 SERVINGS.

Canned Fish

SALMON STEW

1 1-pound can salmon
3/4 cup chopped onion
1/2 cup chopped green pepper
1 clove garlic, finely chopped
1/4 cup margarine
1 chicken bouillon cube
1 cup water
1 1-pound can tomatoes
1 8-ounce can whole-kernel corn
1 cup cooked sliced okra (optional)
1/2 teaspoon salt
1/4 teaspoon thyme
Dash of pepper
1 bay leaf

Drain salmon, reserving 1/3 cup liquid, and break into pieces. In a saucepan, cook onion, green pepper and garlic in margarine until tender and golden. Add salmon, reserved salmon liquid and remaining ingredients. Bring to boil and simmer 15 minutes. Remove bay leaf.

6 SERVINGS.

CREAMED TUNA

1 1½-ounce package dry cream of mushroom
   soup mix
⅓ cup dry milk
1½ cups water
1 6½-ounce can tuna
1 teaspoon freeze-dried parsley

Mix mushroom soup mix and dry milk in a saucepan; gradually stir in water. Drain tuna and rinse to remove oil. Add tuna and parsley to mushroom sauce and cook over medium heat about 5 minutes, stirring. Serve on toast or with rice.

4 SERVINGS.

CLAM-CHOWDERED POTATO SCALLOP

1 7- to 8-ounce can minced clams
1 package Betty Crocker Scalloped Potatoes
3 tablespoons dry milk
3 cups liquid (water plus liquor drained
   from clams)

Drain clams, reserving liquor. Empty scalloped potatoes into skillet and add dry milk; sprinkle in the contents of seasoned sauce mix packet. Add liquid; heat to boiling. Cover and simmer 30 to 35 minutes. Stir in clams; heat through.

4 SERVINGS.

QUICK JAMBALAYA

2 cups instant rice
2 cups water
2 tablespoons onion flakes
2 tablespoons green pepper flakes
1 teaspoon salt
Dash of pepper
Dash of cayenne (or more, to taste)
2 8-ounce cans tomato sauce
1 cup chopped cooked ham
2 4½-ounce cans shrimp, rinsed and drained
1 bay leaf, crumbled

Mix all ingredients in a skillet. Bring to a boil and simmer, uncovered, for 10 minutes, stirring occasionally.
6 SERVINGS.

NOTE: This may also be cooked in foil. Make 2 pouches of double thickness heavy-duty aluminum foil and put half the mixture in each. Cook in coals 15 minutes.

SHRIMP GUMBO

1 10½-ounce can condensed chicken gumbo soup
1 soup can water
½ teaspoon thyme
1 cup cooked sliced okra
2 5-ounce cans broken shrimp, rinsed and drained

Heat soup with water in a saucepan. Add remaining ingredients. Cover and simmer 10 minutes.
4 TO 6 SERVINGS.

QUICK PAELLA

$\frac{1}{4}$ cup margarine
$1\frac{1}{3}$ cups instant rice
$\frac{1}{2}$ cup minced onion
$\frac{1}{3}$ cup minced green pepper
2 cloves garlic, minced
$1\frac{1}{2}$ cups water
2 8-ounce cans tomato sauce
1 7- to 8-ounce can minced clams, drained
1 5-ounce can cooked chicken
Pinch of saffron

Heat margarine in skillet and lightly brown rice, onion, green pepper and garlic. Add remaining ingredients and mix well. Bring to a boil; lower heat and simmer 5 minutes.

4 TO 6 SERVINGS.

NOTE: "Paella" is a gypsy contraction of the Spanish words "para ella"—"for her." Knowing this little gem makes the dish taste even better, somehow.

SOUPS

Soup is liquid with a lot of food power. It can be a meal in itself, an apéritif or even a dessert. Canned and packaged soup mixes are easy to use and delicious, too—especially when you add a touch of your own magic.

Hearty Enough to Make a Meal

EXTRA-RICH MUSHROOM SOUP

1 pound mushrooms
¼ cup margarine
1 cup Campers' Roux (page 37) or
    ¼ cup Gold Medal Flour mixed with
    ⅔ cup dry milk
5 chicken bouillon cubes
3 cups water
1 5-ounce can boned chicken, finely chopped
1 teaspoon marjoram
1 teaspoon Worcestershire sauce
Salt and pepper to taste

Wash, drain, and chop mushrooms into random-sized pieces. Melt margarine in a saucepan; add mushrooms and cook over medium-high heat about 10 minutes, shaking pan and stirring occasionally. Sprinkle roux or combination of flour and dry milk over mushrooms and stir to blend with pan juice.

Add bouillon cubes and water to mushrooms. Stir until soup is thickened and smooth. Add chicken and seasonings; heat through.

4 TO 6 SERVINGS.

MINESTRONE PRONTO

4 slices bacon, chopped, or 2 ounces
   salt pork
3 cups water
1 1½-ounce package dry onion soup mix
½ cup Betty Crocker Potato Buds
1 8-ounce can tomato sauce
½ teaspoon garlic powder
¼ cup green pepper flakes
1 1-pound can kidney beans
Grated Parmesan cheese

In a large saucepan or kettle, fry bacon or salt pork until crisp. Pour off excess fat. Add water; bring to a boil. Add onion soup mix and simmer, uncovered, 10 to 15 minutes.

Remove from heat. Stir in Potato Buds. Add tomato sauce, garlic powder, pepper flakes and beans. Return to heat and simmer 5 minutes longer. Serve with a sprinkle of grated Parmesan cheese.

6 SERVINGS.

SOPA DE ARROZ

2 tablespoons oil
½ cup chopped onion
1 clove garlic, whole but peeled
1½ cups instant rice
1 28-ounce can tomatoes
1 10½-ounce can beef consommé

Heat oil in saucepan and sauté onion and garlic until onion is tender. Discard garlic. Add rice and stir until lightly browned. Add tomatoes and consommé. Bring to a boil; simmer, uncovered, 5 to 10 minutes.

6 TO 8 SERVINGS.

EGG-DROP CHICKEN SOUP

2 10½-ounce cans chicken broth
2 soup cans water
1 cup canned or frozen (thawed) green peas
1 4-ounce can mushroom stems and pieces
  (including liquid)
2 eggs

Mix canned chicken broth and water in a saucepan. Bring to boil. Add peas and mushrooms. Beat eggs till foamy. Pour into simmering broth, stirring with a fork so that eggs cook in tiny strips.

6 TO 8 SERVINGS.

CANADIAN CHEESE SOUP

1 13¾-ounce can chicken broth or 3 chicken
  bouillon cubes dissolved in 1⅔ cups hot
  water
1 package Betty Crocker Au Gratin Potatoes
3 cups water
¼ cup finely diced carrots
¼ cup finely diced celery
½ cup light cream or milk
Freeze-dried parsley

Mix chicken broth or bouillon, potato slices, packet of cheese sauce mix, water, carrots and celery in a large saucepan. Heat to boiling, stirring occasionally. Reduce heat and cover. Simmer about 25 minutes or until potatoes are tender, stirring occasionally. Remove from heat; stir in cream or milk. Garnish with parsley.

6 TO 8 SERVINGS.

BEAN SOUP WITH FRANKS

2 tablespoons oil
2 onions, sliced
1 clove garlic, sliced
3 carrots, sliced
3 cups water
3 cups cooked pinto beans (2 15-ounce cans)
1 teaspoon thyme
1 teaspoon salt
Dash of Worcestershire sauce
4 frankfurters, cut into 1-inch slices

Heat oil in saucepan or kettle; gently sauté onions, garlic and carrots until tender, about 10 minutes. Add water, beans and seasonings. Bring to boil and simmer 15 to 20 minutes. Add frankfurters and heat through.

6 SERVINGS.

QUICK-TRICK CLAM CHOWDER

1 7- to 8-ounce can minced clams
Boiling water
1 package Betty Crocker Scalloped Potatoes
2½ cups milk or 2 cups water plus ¾ cup
   dry milk
1 tablespoon margarine

Open clams and drain, pouring liquor into measuring cup. Add enough boiling water to clam liquor to measure 3 cups. In a large saucepan, mix potato slices, packet of seasoned sauce mix and water-clam liquor mixture. Heat to boiling, stirring occasionally. Reduce heat; cover and simmer about 25 minutes or until potatoes are tender, stirring occasionally. Stir in clams, milk and margarine; heat through.

6 SERVINGS.

Cold Soups for Warm Days

VICHYSSOISE

1 tablespoon onion flakes
3 chicken bouillon cubes
1 cup water
$\frac{1}{4}$ teaspoon salt
$\frac{2}{3}$ cup dry milk
$1\frac{1}{2}$ cups water
$1\frac{1}{4}$ cups Betty Crocker Potato Buds
1 $1\frac{1}{2}$-ounce package sour cream sauce mix
3 tablespoons dry milk
3 tablespoons water
1 tablespoon freeze-dried chives

Combine onion flakes, bouillon cubes, 1 cup water and the salt in a large saucepan. Heat to boiling; cover and simmer 10 minutes. Remove from heat. Mix $\frac{2}{3}$ cup dry milk with $1\frac{1}{2}$ cups water to make 2 cups reconstituted milk. Add $\frac{1}{2}$ cup of this to soup base.

Stir in Potato Buds and whip with a fork till fluffy. Gradually add remaining milk and heat again just to boiling. Cool, then pour into plastic container. Cover and chill. At serving time, mix sour cream sauce mix, 3 tablespoons dry milk and 3 tablespoons water; stir in freeze-dried chives. Add to cold soup and serve.

4 TO 6 SERVINGS.

DESSERT SOUP

1 3-ounce package egg custard mix
¾ cup dry milk
2 cups water
1 8-ounce can sweet cherries
½ teaspoon cinnamon
Dash of nutmeg

In a saucepan, combine custard mix and dry milk. Add water, cherries (including syrup) and spices. Bring quickly to a boil, stirring constantly. Cool, then chill. Serve in bowls or cups.

4 TO 6 SERVINGS.

GAZPACHO

1 clove garlic, minced
1 teaspoon basil
2 tablespoons freeze-dried chives
2 tablespoons freeze-dried parsley
3 tablespoons olive oil or salad oil
1 green pepper, minced
2 cups fresh tomato wedges, peeled
  (3 large tomatoes)
2 tablespoons lemon juice or vinegar
1 small onion, thinly sliced
1 cup chopped cucumber (1 medium cucumber)
1¼ cups ice water
Salt and pepper to taste
Croutons

Mash garlic with herbs and oil. Add green pepper. Mash together with tomato wedges, using a swizzler or potato masher. Mix in lemon juice or vinegar, onion slices, cucumber, ice water, salt and pepper. Chill in a covered plastic container about 4 hours. Serve with croutons.

4 SERVINGS.

Nifty Tricks with Canned and Packaged Soups

Rarebit Soup: Mix a can of tomato soup, a can of Cheddar cheese soup, a can of milk and a can of water. Serve with croutons.

Watercress Soup: To chicken-noodle soup made from a packaged mix add 1 cup watercress leaves.

Floating Islands: Make sour cream sauce from packaged mix, or use real dairy sour cream. Float a generous spoonful on each serving of potato, tomato or other soup.

Seafood Bisque: To 1 can tomato soup, 1 can cream of chicken soup and 2 cans water, add 1 $4\frac{1}{2}$-ounce can broken shrimp, lobster or crabmeat and 1 tablespoon sweet pepper flakes.

Meat-Strip Soup: Make vegetable soup from a packaged mix. Cut Chinese Jerky, salami or cooked ham into thin strips and add a handful or more.

Hot Dog Pea Soup: Make split pea soup from a packaged mix. Add chopped frankfurters or canned Vienna sausage.

Shrimp Soup: If you can find dried shrimp (available in Oriental groceries), add a handful to chicken-noodle soup or chicken broth. Simmer 20 minutes.

VEGETABLES AND SALADS

For campers, vegetables can be canned, dehydrated or even frozen. There are all sorts of ways to vary, combine and dress them up without adding much in the way of time and effort. Still, what would the meals of summer be without vegetables fresh from the field? When you're dealing with a campfire, foil packets are a new wrinkle in vegetable cooking.

Vegetables

STRING BEANS IN FOIL

1 pound fresh string beans, stemmed and
　broken into 1-inch pieces (about 3 cups)
1 clove garlic, peeled and slivered
1 teaspoon rosemary leaves
2 tablespoons margarine
2 cups water
2 teaspoons salt

Make 2 pouches of double thickness heavy-duty aluminum foil. Put half the ingredients—beans, garlic, rosemary leaves, margarine, water and salt—in each. Seal and lay on coals. Cook 25 to 35 minutes, turning once during cooking.

6 SERVINGS.

NOTE: With canned string beans, simply add these seasonings directly to the opened can and heat.

SWEET-SOUR RED CABBAGE

1 medium-sized head red cabbage
3 tablespoons bacon fat
¼ cup chopped onion
¼ cup red wine vinegar
¼ cup sugar
Salt and pepper to taste

Wash and chop cabbage. Melt bacon fat in a skillet; add cabbage and onion, then mix lightly. Cover and cook over low heat 20 minutes. Add remaining ingredients; cover again and cook 10 minutes longer.

6 SERVINGS.

CABBAGE IN FOIL

1 medium-sized head cabbage
1 cup dairy sour cream
1/4 cup dry milk
1/2 cup water
2 teaspoons chopped pimiento
1 teaspoon salt
4 teaspoons onion flakes
1/4 cup grated Parmesan cheese

Wash cabbage and cut into 6 wedges. Place each wedge on a double thickness of heavy-duty aluminum foil, about 14 inches square. In a bowl, mix the sour cream, dry milk, water, pimiento, salt, onion flakes and Parmesan cheese. Spoon over cabbage pieces. Wrap, seal, and lay on coals. Cook 20 to 30 minutes, turning once.

6 SERVINGS.

GRILLED SWEET CARROT STICKS

8 to 10 large carrots
2 tablespoons margarine
1/2 teaspoon salt
Dash of pepper
1/4 cup brown sugar

Cut carrots lengthwise into sticks. Place on double thickness of heavy-duty aluminum foil. Add margarine, salt and pepper. Wrap in foil and seal. Roast on medium coals 30 to 40 minutes or on grill 3 inches from hot coals 1 hour or until soft. Just before serving, sprinkle brown sugar over hot carrots. The heat of the carrots will melt the sugar.

6 SERVINGS.

SUCCOTASH

1 1-pound, 1-ounce can lima beans (2 cups)
1 tablespoon margarine
1 cup cooked or canned corn, drained
1 teaspoon onion flakes
2 teaspoons chopped pimiento
2 tablespoons coffee-"creaming" powder
Salt and pepper to taste

Drain lima beans, reserving ½ cup liquid. Melt margarine in saucepan. Add lima beans, corn, onion flakes, pimiento and reserved liquid. Heat to the boiling point and simmer 10 minutes. Stir in the creaming powder, salt and pepper.

6 SERVINGS.

SQUAW CORN

4 slices bacon
1 medium green pepper, chopped
1 small onion, chopped
1 1-pound can cream-style corn
1 teaspoon salt
Dash of pepper
4 eggs, beaten

Fry bacon until crisp; drain on paper towels. Pour off all but about 3 tablespoons bacon drippings from skillet. Cook and stir green pepper and onion in drippings until onion is tender. Add remaining ingredients. Cook and stir until eggs are thickened throughout but still moist. Crumble bacon over all.

4 TO 6 SERVINGS.

ROAST CORN IN HUSKS

Pull back husks from corn ears and remove silk. Spread corn with margarine. Sprinkle with water and pull husks back over ears. Tie with fine wire or with a strip of husk. Roast on grill 3 inches from hot coals 20 to 30 minutes, turning frequently. Serve at once with salt, pepper and margarine.

CORN IN FOIL

Fresh whole ears of corn
Margarine
Salt and pepper
Water

Remove husks and silk from corn. Generously "butter" corn and place each ear on a separate double thickness of heavy-duty aluminum foil. Sprinkle with salt and pepper and add 2 tablespoons water to each packet. Seal packets and twist ends. Place on coals and cook 20 to 30 minutes, turning once.

EGGPLANT KABOBS

1 medium-sized eggplant
½ cup bottled Italian salad dressing
2 tablespoons catsup
2 tablespoons grated Parmesan cheese

Peel eggplant; cut into 1-inch slices, then into cubes. Mix salad dressing, catsup and Parmesan cheese. Pour over eggplant cubes and let marinate for 30 minutes. Thread onto skewers or green sticks. Cook over hot coals about 20 minutes, rotating to reach all surfaces.
6 TO 8 SERVINGS.

CHEESE-STUFFED PEPPERS

4 medium-sized green peppers
2 tablespoons margarine
½ cup chopped celery
2 cups croutons
1 cup shredded American cheese
1 teaspoon salt

Remove stems and seeds from peppers and parboil in enough water to cover for 5 minutes; drain. Heat margarine in a skillet and sauté celery until tender. Mix in croutons, cheese and salt. Stuff peppers with this mixture; put them back in the skillet. Pour in water to ½-inch depth; bring to boil, cover and simmer 30 minutes.
4 SERVINGS.

TOSS-COOKED VEGETABLES

Anyone who has savored vegetables in a good Chinese restaurant remembers them fondly. The secret, of course, is *very* quick cooking in a small amount of hot oil. With the tougher vegetables, there's a little steaming with broth, soy sauce or sweet-sour sauce.

Choose the leafy vegetables—spinach, Swiss chard, dandelion or mustard greens—and peas, celery, asparagus, green peppers and mushrooms. Combinations are good, too. Whatever the vegetable, cut it diagonally into 1-inch slices. (Don't cut spinach—or, naturally, peas.)

Heat 2 to 3 tablespoons oil in the skillet over high heat. Add the vegetable and stir for about 2 minutes. If and when necessary, pour in liquid (chicken broth or a combination of soy sauce and water—about ½ cup) and stir 2 to 3 minutes longer. You may thicken the pan juice by stirring in a paste of 1 teaspoon cornstarch and 1 teaspoon water. Season to taste and serve immediately!

FOIL-GRILLED ZUCCHINI

4 zucchini (about 1 pound in all)
Salt and pepper
Grated Parmesan cheese
Margarine
4 tablespoons water

Wash zucchini and trim off ends; slice zucchini into
¼-inch rounds. Make 4 squares, about 14 inches each, of
double thickness heavy-duty aluminum foil. Place 1
zucchini—in slices—on each square. Sprinkle with salt,
pepper and Parmesan cheese. Add a dab of margarine and
1 tablespoon water to each serving and seal. Cook on the
coals about 15 minutes, turning once.
   4 SERVINGS.

NOTE: This treatment is also good with yellow crookneck
squash and summer squash.

SKILLET-SCALLOPED TOMATOES

2 tablespoons margarine
1 cup croutons or ¾ cup crumbled soda crackers
1 1-pound can tomatoes or 2 cups chopped
   peeled fresh tomatoes
1½ teaspoons dried basil
½ teaspoon salt
Pepper to taste

Melt margarine in skillet. Add croutons or crumbs,
tomatoes and seasonings. Simmer, uncovered, 20 minutes.
Very tasty with grilled veal, fish or scrambled eggs.
   4 SERVINGS.

NOTE: If you have Pesto Sauce (page 36), substitute 1½
teaspoons for the dried basil.

COUNTRY-FRIED TOMATOES

3 large, firm tomatoes
Bisquick or flour seasoned with salt and pepper
3 tablespoons bacon drippings or oil
2 tablespoons flour
1 cup milk

Cut off stem and blossom ends of tomatoes and slice about ½ inch thick. Dredge tomatoes in seasoned Bisquick or flour. Heat drippings or oil in skillet and sauté tomato slices until browned on both sides. Remove from pan. To make gravy, stir the 2 tablespoons flour into the fat left in the pan, add milk and stir until thickened. Season to taste with more salt and pepper and pour over tomatoes.
4 SERVINGS.

NOTE: Here's the place for Campers' Roux (page 37). Instead of making gravy with flour and milk, mix ½ cup Campers' Roux with fat in pan, add 1 cup water, and stir until . . . well, you know.

POTATOES IN FOIL

Choose medium-sized sweet potatoes, yams or white baking potatoes. Scrub potatoes and rub skins with oil, bacon fat or margarine. Wrap each potato in heavy-duty aluminum foil. Roast on medium-hot coals 45 to 60 minutes or on grill about 3 inches from hot coals about 1 hour, turning frequently. Potatoes are done when soft to touch with (gloved!) thumb.

To serve, make crosswise slits through foil and potato, fold back foil and squeeze gently until potato pops up through opening. Serve sweets or yams with margarine and brown sugar, white potatoes with margarine and chives or sour cream sauce made from packaged mix.

SOUR CREAM MASHED POTATOES

Prepare Betty Crocker Potato Buds for 8 servings as directed on package except—stir in $1\frac{1}{2}$-ounce package sour cream sauce mix with the Potato Buds. If desired, sprinkle potatoes with paprika or freeze-dried chives.

8 SERVINGS.

FOILED RICE CASSEROLE

$1\frac{1}{3}$ cups instant rice
1 4-ounce can mushroom stems and pieces,
    drained, or $\frac{1}{4}$ cup dried mushrooms
1 tablespoon onion flakes
$\frac{1}{2}$ teaspoon salt
Dash of cayenne pepper
2 tablespoons margarine
$1\frac{1}{3}$ cups water (with canned mushrooms, use 1 cup
    water and $\frac{1}{3}$ cup mushroom liquid)

Tear 2 pieces of heavy-duty aluminum foil from a 14-inch roll and place them, one on top of the other, in a bowl or saucepan. Pour in the rice. Mix mushrooms, onion flakes, seasonings, margarine and water. (If using dried mushrooms, let stand 10 to 15 minutes.) Pour the liquid mixture over the rice and mix well.

Seal the foil pouch by rolling the top, allowing a little room for expansion during cooking. Place the package on the coals and cook 20 to 25 minutes; occasionally pick it up with tongs and give it a shake.

4 SERVINGS.

Salads

MARINATED VEGETABLE SALAD

Open cans of vegetables and pour off liquid, leaving the vegetables in the cans. Pour in a well-seasoned oil-and-vinegar dressing of your own design (2 parts oil to 1 part vinegar, with salt, pepper and thyme or marjoram to taste) or a bottled Italian dressing to cover vegetables. Marinate 8 hours or more. At serving time, mix the drained vegetables; add fresh tomatoes, cucumbers and/or salad greens if you like.

Good vegetables for this treatment are string beans (especially the dill-flavored kind), asparagus, carrots, beets, garbanzos and mushrooms.

NOTE: Beets are a wonderful salad ingredient, but do use some discretion about what sort of color combination you make with them.

WILTED SALAD

4 slices bacon, chopped
½ cup chopped onion
¼ cup vinegar
1 quart bite-size pieces of leaf lettuce,
　　raw spinach, sorrel or
　　dandelion greens
Salt and pepper to taste

Cook bacon pieces and onion in a skillet until bacon is crisp and onion is tender and golden. Add vinegar and bring to a boil. Add greens and toss with hot dressing until wilted. (Or cover skillet and remove from heat; let greens stand about 5 minutes.) Season to taste.
4 SERVINGS.

SALSA

1 14½-ounce can sliced baby tomatoes
3 canned green chili peppers, seeded and
   chopped
1 tablespoon vinegar
1 tablespoon sugar
½ cup chopped onion
1 teaspoon salt
¼ teaspoon black pepper

Mix all ingredients. Let stand at least 30 minutes or until the rest of the meal is ready to serve.
4 TO 6 SERVINGS.

NOTE: This is especially good with bean dishes such as Sunflower Chili (page 71), canned tamales or tacos.

COLESLAW

5 cups finely chopped cabbage (1 small head)
1 teaspoon salt
1 tablespoon sugar
1 tablespoon vinegar
1 teaspoon prepared mustard
⅓ cup mayonnaise
1 tablespoon sweet pickle relish

Mix all ingredients. Serve cold.
4 TO 6 SERVINGS.

FRESH PICKLES

4 large cucumbers
2 teaspoons salt
3 green onions, finely sliced
$\frac{1}{2}$ cup vinegar
3 tablespoons cold water
2 teaspoons sugar
$\frac{1}{4}$ teaspoon pepper

Peel cucumbers and slice thinly. Layer in a bowl with the salt and let stand 30 minutes. Drain thoroughly. Add sliced green onions. Mix vinegar, water, sugar and pepper; pour over the cucumbers. Serve cold.

8 SERVINGS.

SOLIANKA

1 1-pound can sauerkraut
1 Bermuda onion, peeled and thinly sliced
2 dill pickles, cut into slivers
1 firm tart apple, peeled and cut into
    thin slices
$\frac{1}{4}$ pound cooked ham, canned luncheon
    meat or Chinese Barbecued Pork (page 35),
    cut into slivers

Drain sauerkraut, reserving liquid. Place about a third of the sauerkraut in a bowl and top with a few slices of onion, a few slivers of pickle, a few slices of apple, and top with a sprinkling of slivers of meat. Repeat, making 3 layers. Pour reserved sauerkraut liquid over all. Let stand about 1 hour. A fine side dish with barbecued meat.

6 SERVINGS.

QUICK ZUCCHINI SALAD

Into a bowl, cut zucchini into thin slices. (Figure on 1 small zucchini per person.) Sprinkle with freeze-dried parsley. Add bottled Italian dressing or oil and vinegar and toss gently.

TOMATOES WITH HERBS

About an hour before eating, peel and slice tomatoes. Sprinkle with a mixture of dried thyme and basil, then with salt and pepper. Drizzle red wine vinegar over the tomato slices. Cover lightly and let stand in a cool place. The herb flavors will seep into the tomatoes.

HOT GERMAN POTATO SALAD

4 slices bacon
1 package Betty Crocker Scalloped Potatoes
3 cups water
3 to 4 tablespoons vinegar
1 hard-cooked egg

In large skillet, fry bacon until crisp; drain on paper towels and crumble bacon. Drain drippings from skillet, reserving 3 tablespoons. Empty potato slices and packet of seasoned sauce mix into skillet; stir in water. Heat to boiling. Cover and simmer 25 minutes or until potatoes are tender, stirring occasionally. Carefully stir in vinegar, bacon and the 3 tablespoons bacon drippings. Garnish with finely chopped hard-cooked egg.

6 SERVINGS.

GOOD AND EASY POTATO SALAD

1 package Betty Crocker Scalloped Potatoes
3 cups water
2 tablespoons oil
$\frac{2}{3}$ cup water
2 tablespoons vinegar (tarragon, if possible)
$\frac{1}{4}$ cup mayonnaise or salad dressing
1 teaspoon prepared mustard
$\frac{1}{2}$ cup diced celery
2 hard-cooked eggs, chopped

Empty potato slices into saucepan. Add 3 cups water. Heat to boiling; reduce heat and simmer until tender, 15 to 20 minutes. Rinse with cold water and drain thoroughly. Place in bowl; cover and chill.

In saucepan, mix the packet of seasoned sauce mix with oil and stir in $\frac{2}{3}$ cup water and the vinegar. Heat to boiling over medium heat, stirring constantly. Cover and chill. Blend mayonnaise and mustard into sauce. Combine potatoes, celery and eggs; fold in sauce.

6 SERVINGS.

BREADS

You may not have a thermostatically controlled oven in your camping outfit, but you do have a grill, skillet, maybe a reflector oven . . . the better to make biscuits, hush puppies and other quick breads. Furthermore, it's easy to vary bakers' goods and turn them into delectable tidbits.

Brought-Along Breads

GARLIC FRENCH BREAD

Peel and mince 1 or 2 cloves of garlic. Crush them in a bowl and mix in $\frac{1}{2}$ cup butter or margarine.

Cut a 1-pound loaf of French bread in $\frac{3}{4}$- to 1-inch-thick slices, not cutting quite all the way through the bottom crust. Spread each slice with garlic butter and press loaf into its original shape. Wrap in heavy-duty aluminum foil. Place on grill or beside (not in) coals. Heat 15 to 20 minutes, turning once.

HERB BUTTERS

To the garlic butter in the recipe above, add and mix in 1 teaspoon freeze-dried parsley and/or one of the following herbs:

> 1 teaspoon basil
> 1 teaspoon marjoram
> $\frac{1}{2}$ teaspoon oregano

CROUTON CLUSTERS

> 2 cups croutons
> 2 cups shredded American cheese

Lightly toss croutons with cheese to mix. Form into 1-inch balls, packing so they'll hold together. Use as a soup garnish, or lightly fry in margarine or bacon fat and eat with catsup.

MAKES 16 TO 20.

ENGLISH MUFFIN PIZZA

4 English muffins
Sliced salami or drained anchovies
Mozzarella or Swiss cheese, cut into
    thin slices
1 10½-ounce can pizza sauce, warmed

Split each English muffin in half; brush split sides with oil. Heat and toast muffin halves. On each split side, arrange salami or anchovies and cheese. Pour pizza sauce over each and cook in reflector oven or in covered skillet on grill until cheese softens and sauce is heated.
MAKES 8.

CHEESE FLOATS

Arrange thin slices of American or Swiss cheese on crisp-toasted slices of rye bread. Float in onion soup at serving time.

ROLL BOATS

Use French dinner rolls with thick, crisp crusts. The ones shaped like little footballs are good, as are the ones shaped like bed pillows. Slice off the top crust and hollow out with a fork. Toast inside surface lightly and brush with melted butter or margarine. Fill with any creamed vegetable or meat, or any savory stew or hash.

NOTE: The bread removed from the rolls can be shredded, lightly toasted, and used like croutons.

Breads Baked in Camp

BREAD ON A STICK

Prepare Biscuit dough as directed on Bisquick package. Have green sticks ready; bark should be stripped from cooking end. Form dough into balls about 1 inch in diameter and spear onto ends of sticks. Hold over medium coals, first about 6 inches from coals to cook dough, then closer to brown; keep turning so all sides will be evenly done. Serve with margarine.

MAKES 24.

OR: make strips about 4 inches long and twist around sticks ribbon-fashion. Cook as above.

SKILLET BISCUITS

Prepare Biscuit dough as directed on Bisquick package. Melt ¼ cup butter or margarine in 10-inch skillet. Sprinkle with onion salt, garlic salt and paprika. Roll or pat dough ½ inch thick and cut into 12 biscuits. (There's no law that says biscuits must be round, you know.) Arrange in skillet, turning biscuits to coat both sides with seasoned butter. Cover skillet (use heavy-duty aluminum foil if you don't have a lid). Place on grill 4 inches from hot coals. Bake 10 minutes; check to see biscuits aren't getting burned. You may want to cook them 5 minutes longer or until done. Invert onto serving plate. Serve hot.

MAKES 12.

SKILLET CORN BREAD

No matter what you call it—Johnny Cake, *Journey* Cake, Spider Bread (baked in a skillet with legs, hence a spider) or Hoecake (baked on the blade of a hoe)—this bread is the food of ingenious and hungry people: hunters, trappers, fishermen, farmers. . . . and maybe you.

    1 cup cornmeal
    1 teaspoon salt
    1 teaspoon sugar
    1¼ cups boiling water
    Oil or bacon fat

Combine cornmeal, salt and sugar; stir in boiling water. Heat skillet or griddle; grease generously with oil or bacon fat. Drop batter by tablespoonfuls onto hot pan and cook about 5 minutes. Turn and cook 5 minutes longer. Serve immediately. Particularly good with fish.

MAKES 8 TO 10.

HUSH PUPPIES

    2¼ cups yellow cornmeal
    1 teaspoon salt
    2 teaspoons onion flakes
    ¾ teaspoon baking soda
    1½ cups buttermilk
    Oil
    Butter or margarine

In a bowl, mix cornmeal, salt, onion flakes and baking soda. Add buttermilk and mix well. Drop by spoonfuls into hot oil (about 1 inch deep). Cook until well browned, about 2 minutes. Serve immediately with plenty of butter or margarine, cold or melted. Especially good with grilled or fried chicken, fish or shellfish.

MAKES ABOUT 24.

SWEET CINNAMON ROLLS

Prepare Biscuits as directed on Bisquick package and bake as for Skillet Biscuits or in reflector oven—but first roll cut biscuits in a mixture of $\frac{1}{4}$ cup sugar and 1 teaspoon cinnamon (or shake them, one at a time, in a bag with this mixture).

ONION BUTTER BISCUITS

Prepare Biscuit dough as directed on Bisquick package except—add 2 tablespoons dry onion soup mix. Melt $\frac{1}{3}$ cup margarine in 8-inch foil pie plate on grill. Stir in 2 more tablespoons onion soup mix. Pour half of this mixture into another 8-inch foil pie plate. Drop dough by spoonfuls into hot prepared pan. Pour butter mixture from other pan over biscuits; invert pan over pan with biscuits and secure rims together with spring-type clothespins. Place on grill 4 inches from hot coals. Bake 8 to 10 minutes. Remove pans from grill. Turn over and bake 8 to 10 minutes longer.
MAKES 12.

ZEBRA BREAD

Prepare Biscuit dough as directed on Bisquick package except—add $\frac{1}{4}$ cup sesame seed and $\frac{1}{2}$ teaspoon salt. Knead the dough 5 times on a lightly floured surface. Divide dough in half and roll or pat each half into a rectangle, about 12x8 inches. Cut each of these in half. Grill strips 5 inches from medium coals 3 to 4 minutes on each side. Cut each strip into 4 pieces; serve hot with margarine.
MAKES 16.

BEVERAGES

To warm up or cool off, between meals or with them, something special to drink adds the right touch.

The Basic Drinks

COFFEE

You don't need a recipe for instant coffee. Some people actually prefer it to ground coffee. These people will of course take instant coffee camping. It couldn't be easier. It's even easier if you buy the individual-serving-size packages.

Other people don't like instant coffee at all—and they will pack their favorite ground coffee. An inexpensive aluminum percolator travels well; without the coffee basket, it will boil water for any other purpose, too. (It's not a bad idea to get an extra glass top—the little piece that fits into the lid—and take it along in case the original gets lost or broken. Nothing is as useless as a percolator whose little glass lid is missing.)

Old-timers at camping, and sometimes new-timers, hold out for real campfire coffee, rich and strong and (let's face it) a bit cloudy . . . with a few grounds in the bottom of the cup. There are at least two ways to make it, each passionately defended by its advocates.

CAMPFIRE COFFEE I

Heat 2 quarts water to boiling. Meanwhile, mix 1 cup regular-grind coffee, 3 tablespoons cold water and 1 slightly beaten egg. (Purists crush the eggshell and mix that in, too.) Tie loosely in a large cloth bag, leaving a long cord. (Some people think the cloth bag is unnecessary, effete, and a nuisance.) As soon as the water boils, drop the coffee mixture into it—and hang onto the cord. Immediately remove the pot from direct heat and let stand 5 to 10 minutes. Move the sack up and down with the cord. Add ⅓ cup cold water; let stand 3 or 4 minutes longer.
8 CUPS.

CAMPFIRE COFFEE II

In a bail-handled kettle or a 2-pound coffee can (which is handled with a pair of pliers when it's too hot to lift), heat 2 quarts water to boiling. Dump in 1 cup regular-grind coffee. Immediately remove kettle from direct heat and let stand 10 minutes. If you're cooking eggs, crush the shells and dump them in, too. Pour in ½ cup cold water to settle the grounds. Pour coffee carefully into cups.

8 CUPS.

CAFE AU LAIT

Brew 4 cups coffee in the way you prefer. Heat 1 quart milk in a saucepan until bubbles appear at the edges. With both liquids hot, pour them simultaneously into cups. Add sugar and cinnamon, if desired.

8 CUPS.

MOCHA

⅔ cup instant cocoa mix
½ cup instant coffee
8 cups boiling water
Sweetened whipped cream, pressurized
     whipped cream or a substitute made with
     dessert topping mix

Mix cocoa and coffee in a pot or pitcher. Pour in boiling water and stir. Serve hot and top with whipped cream.

8 TO 10 SERVINGS.

NOTE: Children might enjoy this along with the adults if the coffee used is the decaffinated kind.

TEA

Real tea drinkers feel just as strongly about tea as coffee lovers do about *their* beverage. They either defend or strongly oppose tea leaves, tea bags and instant tea. Again, no instructions are needed, unless it's to say that the proportion is 1 teaspoon tea leaves to each cup of boiling water and that the longer it brews the stronger it is (3 minutes is the standard interval).

Dried or fresh mint leaves, ½ teaspoon or more per cup, make tea taste good, I think.

If the tea is to be cooled and iced, add mint and several strips of lemon or orange peel while it's very hot.

YERBA BUENA TEA

Maybe you'll be lucky enough to find some oregano (wild marjoram) on a sunny hillside. Otherwise, use dried oregano. Add 1 teaspoon dried oregano or 2 teaspoons fresh for each cup of boiling water; brew 15 to 20 minutes. Strain off the leaves.

NIPPY ICED TEA

    4 cups boiling water
    4 teaspoons tea leaves
    Peel and juice of ½ lemon
    2 teaspoons dried mint leaves
    1 12-ounce can ginger ale

Pour boiling water over tea leaves, lemon peel and mint leaves. Cool. Strain into pitcher. Add lemon juice and ginger ale. Serve over ice.

4 TO 6 SERVINGS.

Specialties of the Campsite

MILK AND HONEY

To a glass or cup of water add 1 tablespoon honey and stir until dissolved. Add 5 tablespoons dry milk and stir until dissolved.

1 SERVING.

NOTE: Restaurants have honey packaged in one-serving plastic packets. These are handy for hiking and camping.

MULLED CIDER

1 quart apple cider
2 cinnamon sticks or 1 teaspoon
  ground cinnamon
3 whole cloves
$\frac{1}{4}$ cup raisins
$\frac{1}{4}$ cup broken almonds (optional)

Heat cider until bubbles appear at the edge of the pan. Add spices, raisins and almonds. Let steep without boiling 1 hour.

4 SERVINGS.

EGGNOG

For each serving, use . . .

1 egg
1 cup milk
1 tablespoon sugar
Dash of nutmeg

Beat egg and add remaining ingredients. If you like, you may add 1 tablespoon unflavored malted milk powder. Serve immediately.

HOT GEL

Like many other great discoveries, this was an accident. The director of a summer camp for little girls had her charges mix flavored gelatin according to package instructions at night. The idea, of course, was that the gelatin would set during the night for eating next day. The little girls, however, drank it when it was just cool enough—and liked it so well that it became a regular bedtime treat.

Extra touches for various flavors:

- To cherry or raspberry, add two strips of lemon peel.
- To lemon or lime, add a sprig of mint or 1 teaspoon dried mint.

FRUIT PUNCH

1 32-ounce bottle cranberry juice
1 cup orange juice
$\frac{1}{4}$ cup sugar
1 cup water

Mix all ingredients and stir until sugar is dissolved. Serve over ice.

8 SERVINGS.

DESSERTS

*When you're more active than usual and out of doors most of
the time, the sweet tooth gets quite keen; hence, the popular-
ity of standbys like S'Mores and Mock Angel Food. Some
desserts, like Fruit Dumplings, Rice Pudding in Foil and
Gingerbread à l'Orange, have been known to appear at
breakfast in camping circles.*

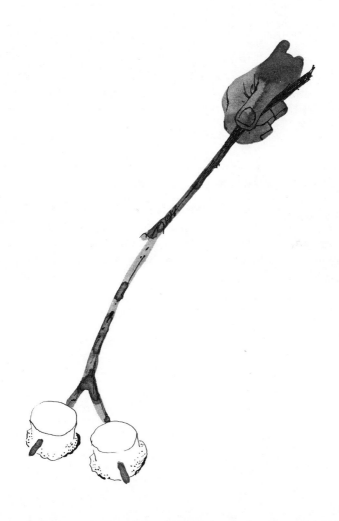

REALLY ROCKY ROADS

1 package Betty Crocker Chocolate
  Fudge Frosting Mix
3 tablespoons margarine, softened
3 to 4 tablespoons hot water
2 cups miniature marshmallows or cut-up large
  marshmallows
1 cup peanuts

In a small bowl, mix frosting mix, margarine and hot water. Beat until creamy, about 1 minute. Stir in marshmallows and peanuts. Line a plate or pan with a sheet of heavy-duty aluminum foil and grease the foil with margarine. Pour mixture onto foil and pat it out "with buttered hands" into a 1½-inch-thick patty. Let stand until firm; cut into squares.

RICE PUDDING IN FOIL

Soak about 1 cup dried apple slices in cold water 30 minutes or longer. When the campfire is a bed of glowing embers, each camper makes his own pudding in a bowl-shaped double thickness of heavy-duty aluminum foil. (You'll need a 14-inch square.)

Then, with . . .

⅓ cup instant rice
⅓ cup water (in which apples have soaked)
2 tablespoons sugar
3 tablespoons apple slices
1 tablespoon raisins
Dash each of salt, cinnamon and nutmeg

Mix all ingredients in foil bowl. Seal foil and lay on coals. Cook 15 minutes.

1 SERVING.

GINGERBREAD A L'ORANGE

Though we list this recipe with desserts, it should be noted that two families who tested it decided it was perfect for breakfast. "First we eat the oranges," they reported, "then . . . "

  8 to 10 large oranges, cut in half
  1 package Betty Crocker Gingerbread Mix
  1 cup water

Carefully remove fruit from orange halves to form orange cups.

Pour gingerbread mix into a bowl; add water and beat about 300 strokes. Pour batter into the orange cups, leaving about ¾ inch at the top to allow for rising. Carefully place the orange cups upright in hot coals. Cook about 12 minutes or until the surfaces of the cakes have lost their sheen. Remove from coals and cool slightly. Garnish with a dab of margarine and eat with a spoon. Allow at least two for each person.

NOTE: Want to divide this recipe in half? Use 4 or 5 large oranges. Measure contents of gingerbread mix package and divide in half (about 1½ cups). Use only ½ cup water and beat about 200 strokes.

CHOCOLATE DUMPLINGS

1 cup brown sugar (packed)
1/3 cup Bisquick
3 cups water
1 6-ounce package semisweet chocolate
  pieces
2 cups Bisquick
2 tablespoons dry milk
1/4 cup granulated sugar
1/2 teaspoon cinnamon
1/2 cup water

Stir together brown sugar and 1/3 cup Bisquick in large heavy skillet. Gradually stir in 3 cups water; add chocolate pieces. Cook over low heat, stirring constantly, until chocolate melts and mixture thickens slightly.

Mix remaining ingredients to a stiff batter. Drop batter by tablespoonfuls into simmering chocolate mixture. Cook 10 minutes uncovered; cover and cook 10 minutes longer. To serve, spoon chocolate mixture over dumplings.

6 TO 8 SERVINGS.

S'MORES

For each serving, place 4 squares of a milk chocolate candy bar on a graham cracker. Toast a marshmallow over campfire; slip onto the chocolate and top with a second graham cracker. Eat like a sandwich.

FRUIT DUMPLINGS

1 1-pound package mixed dried fruits
1 cup raisins
½ cup sugar
1 tablespoon cornstarch
½ teaspoon cinnamon
½ teaspoon nutmeg
4 cups water
1 cup Bisquick
1 tablespoon dry milk
⅓ cup water

In a saucepan, mix dried fruits, raisins, sugar, cornstarch, spices and 4 cups water. Heat to boiling, stirring frequently. Simmer 30 minutes, stirring occasionally, until fruit is tender.

Combine Bisquick and dry milk in a bowl; add ⅓ cup water and stir into a stiff batter. Drop by tablespoonfuls into simmering fruit mixture. Cook uncovered 10 minutes; cover and cook 10 minutes longer. To serve, spoon fruit mixture over the dumplings.

6 TO 8 SERVINGS.

PEACHES IN FOIL

Large fresh peaches
Cinnamon
Currant or blackberry jelly

Wash peaches, cut in half and remove pits. Place each peach half on a double thickness of heavy-duty aluminum foil. Sprinkle with cinnamon. Put 1 teaspoon jelly in pit cavity. Seal foil and lay on coals. Cook about 12 minutes.

BANANA BOATS

For each serving, cut a V-shaped wedge lengthwise in a peeled firm banana. Place on a double thickness of heavy-duty aluminum foil, about 18x6 inches. Fill groove with cut-up or miniature marshmallows and chocolate pieces. Wrap securely in foil. Cook directly on medium coals about 10 minutes.

MOCK ANGEL FOOD

Cut crusts from day-old unsliced loaf of bread; cut into 2-inch cubes. Place bread securely on skewers or pointed green sticks. Dip bread in sweetened condensed milk, then in grated coconut, coating evenly. Toast over medium coals until coconut is brown.

Wherever you are, whatever the season, certain questions will arise while you're adapting and coping.

Building a Cooking Fire

No matter what you plan to cook over a campfire, allow about an hour to get the fire ready. Cooking is done over, on or in the coals—the embers that glow after the flaming, roaring, smoky fire has died down, or when the charcoal has a white ash. The length of time it will take depends on the type and size of wood with which you feed the fire. Hardwoods take longer to burn down than the resinous, pithy wood of conifers, but they also give hotter, longer-lasting coals. Use dry wood and avoid rotten wood, which burns too quickly and doesn't leave much in the way of coals. Charcoal briquets are a good supplement or substitute for a sparse supply of firewood.

If you're in an area where gathering or cutting your own firewood is permitted (best to be sure about this), divide the wood collection into three piles. Group the small twigs for kindling, then sticks about the size of your thumb and finally wood about the diameter of your wrist. Larger logs aren't too practical for cooking fires.

Where to Build the Fire

In campgrounds there are usually fireplaces. If you're in a spot where there is none, make sure the site is safe. Don't build a fire under a tree or over tree roots. Clear the ground of inflammable forest droppings—pine needles, dry leaves, dead grass—all around the spot where the fire will be, and circle the area with rocks or logs. *You will, of course, have checked on whether you need a fire permit, and you will follow the regulations that come with it.*

The fire can be any shape or size; most beginners make a bigger one than they need. Anyhow, start with wads of newspaper, strips from an empty waxed-cardboard carton, pine needles, dry grass or bark; next add a little tee-pee of small twigs. Around or over this (your fire can be shaped like a teepee, an A-frame or a log cabin), go the thumb-sized pieces, and finally the larger pieces. Make sure the fire is well ventilated; you may lay rocks or large logs at the leeward side of the fire so that the wind will act as your bellows (and blow the smoke *away* from you!). Don't try to rush the fire. If you add the large wood too soon, you'll only extinguish your kindling fire.

Windy Weather

Before starting the fire, dig a small trench about 6 inches deep, about a foot wide, and 2 feet or more long. Build your fire in this hole as usual, and lay your grill over it when you're ready to cook.

Pit Cooking

Dig a good-sized hole a foot or so deep and wide enough to hold the food you want to cook. Line it with rocks (check to make sure they're not porous rocks, which might explode with heat) and build a fire as usual. Since the pit is naturally not well-ventilated, getting the fire going is a little more troublesome. Lighting the stub of a candle in the center of the fire helps. When the fire has burned down to coals, rake them back and put in whatever it is you want to cook. Perhaps it's a Dutch oven of seasoned, soaked beans with salt pork. Put the lid upside down on the Dutch oven, pile coals on top, cover it all with dirt or sand, and cook for eight hours. Lobsters or clams over a bed of seaweed or wet newspapers are also naturals for pit cooking. Cover with more seaweed, pile coals on top as before, top with dirt or sand, and let steam for about an hour.

A watchword—if you do build a fire in a trench or pit, be sure to fill the hole before you leave the campsite.

(Here, it might be noted that when Paul Bunyan went into the timberland at the southern end of the Cascades in 1915, *his* cook buried a beanpot and forgot where he put it. The beans boiled over, and there is *still* a steamy, sulphurous area to mark the spot in Lassen National Park. So *do* remember where you dig your pit.)

The Reflector Oven Fire

Find or build a small rock wall. Against the wall build a small fire as usual except that when you lay on the largest pieces of wood, bank them against the rocks. Set up the reflector oven about a foot away. You can begin cooking when the fire is burning brightly. This is the only kind of campfire cooking you do *before* the flames die down.

Cookies and biscuits and their variations can be baked with a reflector oven, but cakes and pies aren't usually successful.

Important!

Don't take chances with your fire! If you want your children and grandchildren to be able to enjoy these campsites, you must do your part to protect and preserve them.

■ Don't go away and leave a campfire burning. When you're through with your fire, extinguish it by drowning, stir the ashes and drown again.

■ Don't leave a campfire burning while you sleep.

■ Make *sure* the fire is out and the embers cool before you leave the site.

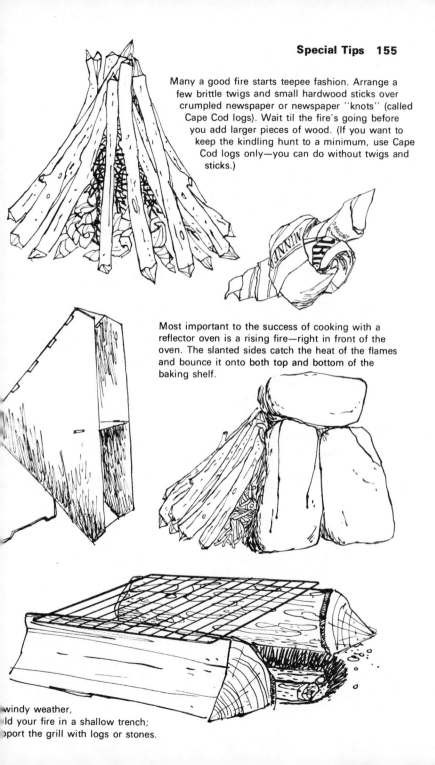

Many a good fire starts teepee fashion. Arrange a few brittle twigs and small hardwood sticks over crumpled newspaper or newspaper "knots" (called Cape Cod logs). Wait til the fire's going before you add larger pieces of wood. (If you want to keep the kindling hunt to a minimum, use Cape Cod logs only—you can do without twigs and sticks.)

Most important to the success of cooking with a reflector oven is a rising fire—right in front of the oven. The slanted sides catch the heat of the flames and bounce it onto both top and bottom of the baking shelf.

windy weather,
ld your fire in a shallow trench;
port the grill with logs or stones.

High Altitudes

At sea level, water boils at 212° Fahrenheit. With each elevation of 500 feet, the boiling temperature is one degree less—202°F., for instance, at 5,000 feet. Allowing for this variation is quite a bit easier in a well-appointed kitchen in Denver or Salt Lake City than in a campground in Tuolumne Meadows or the Pisgah National Forest. Suffice it to say that anything cooked in boiling water seems to take forever in the high-country camps. My solution is to use instant rice instead of the raw kind, to eat canned spaghetti instead of trying to boil it, and not (after a couple of discouraging experiences) to try boiled eggs at all. What altitude does to baked goods need not concern the camp cook; biscuits made with Bisquick are satisfactory without adjustment, and cake baking can be postponed until you get home.

Suppose It Rains

Unless the rainfall is an absolutely drenching downpour, you can take shelter under a tarp or tent flap to set up the camp stove and construct the uncooked part of the meal inside your tent, camper or station wagon. If the rain is heavy and unlikely to let up for many hours, I think the only thing to do is—as my husband says—show the white feather: pack up and seek shelter in a nice, dry, comfortable motel.

Beach Camping

Delightful as beach camping is, it has three distinct hazards: sand, devastating heat from the sun through the middle of the day, and—when the sea breezes fail—insects. For comfortable cooking and eating and less sandy food, a table and campstools are rather more essential here than in other camping spots. For beach camping, two ice chests are better than one. Be sure the family is well supplied with insect repellent to ward off mosquitoes and gnats. Cover food while preparing and eating meals with cloths or net tents.

Good Campkeeping Tips

Burn all combustible garbage—cartons, wrappers, paper plates and cups, napkins and so on. What won't burn should of course be carefully disposed of. Just as you're pleased to find that the last party left the site neat, so will the next party be pleased with *you!*

Rinse out metal cans, remove both ends and flatten. Discard in garbage cans, if there are any, or bury. Also bury the foil used for wrapping or cooking.

Before you dump dishwater, consider that it's laden with food particles which will attract ants, wasps and other unpleasant visitors. Find or dig a small trench, pour out the dishwater and cover with sand, dirt or forest duff.

Home Again

Isn't the kitchen sink beautiful? You can get hot water by merely twisting a faucet! And the refrigerator—it makes its own ice! And the oven—you can bake and roast and broil to your heart's content! And the garbage disposal, and the dishwasher. . . .

But didn't the food you prepared so ingeniously taste marvelous? And wasn't it fun?

INDEX